The Americans with Disabilities Act Handbook

Maureen Harrison
Steve Gilbert
Editors

EXCELLENT BOOKS
BEVERLY HILLS, CALIFORNIA

R
346.7301
Ad 11 a

EXCELLENT BOOKS
Post Office Box 7121
Beverly Hills, CA 90212-7121

Publisher's Cataloging in Publication Data

The ADA Handbook/
 Maureen Harrison, Steve Gilbert, editors.
 p. cm. - (Landmark Laws Series)
Bibliography:p.
Includes Index.
1. Handicapped - Employment - Law and Legislation -
United States - Handbooks
I. Title. II. Harrison, Maureen. III. Gilbert, Steve.
IV. Series: Landmark Laws.
KF480 A32 1992   LC 92-72951
344.0159 A 1992 - dc20

ISBN 1-880780-00-3
ISBN 1-880780-01-1 (Landmark Laws Series)

Table of Contents

MAUREEN HARRISON is a textbook editor

STEVE GILBERT is a law librarian

They are the editors of the Landmark Decisions Series
and the Landmark Laws Series

STATEMENT BY PRESIDENT GEORGE BUSH
UPON SIGNING THE
AMERICANS WITH DISABILITIES ACT OF 1990

Today, I am signing S. 933, the "Americans with Disabilities Act of 1990." In this extraordinary year, we have seen our own Declaration of Independence inspire the march of freedom throughout Eastern Europe. It is altogether fitting that the American people have once again given clear expression to our most basic ideals of freedom and equality. The Americans with Disabilities Act represents the full flowering of our democratic principles, and it gives me great pleasure to sign it into law today.

In 1986, on behalf of President Reagan, I personally accepted a report from the National Council on Disability entitled "Toward Independence." In that report, the National Council recommended the enactment of comprehensive legislation to ban discrimination against persons with disabilities. The Americans with Disabilities Act (ADA) is such legislation. It promises to open up all aspects of American life to individuals with disabilities - employment opportunities, government services, public accommodations, transportation, and telecommunications.

This legislation is comprehensive because the barriers faced by individuals with disabilities are wide-ranging. Existing laws and regulations under the Rehabilitation Act of 1973 have been effective with respect to the Federal Government, its contractors, and the recipients of Federal funds. However, they have left broad areas of American life untouched or inadequately addressed. Many of our young people, who have benefited from the equal educational opportunity guaranteed under the Rehabilitation Act and the Education of the Handicapped Act, have found themselves on graduation day still shut out of the mainstream of American life. They have faced persistent discrimination in the workplace and barriers posed by inaccessible public transportation, public accommodations, and telecommunications.

Fears that the ADA is too vague or too costly and will lead to an explosion of litigation are misplaced. The Administration worked closely with the Congress to ensure that, wherever possible, existing language and standards from the Rehabilitation Act were incorporated into the ADA. The Rehabilitation Act standards are already familiar to large segments of the private sector that are either Federal contractors or recipients of Federal funds. Because the Rehabilitation Act was enacted 17 years ago, there is already an extensive body of law interpreting the requirements of that Act. Employers can turn to these interpretations for guidance on how to meet their obligations under the ADA.

The Administration and the Congress have carefully crafted the ADA to give the business community the flexibility to meet the requirements of the Act without incurring undue costs. Cost may be taken into account in determining how an employee is "reasonably accommodated," whether the removal of a barrier is "readily achievable," or whether the provision of a particular auxiliary aid would result in an "undue burden." The ADA's most rigorous access requirements are reserved for new construction where the added costs of accessible features are minimal in relation to overall construction costs. An elevator exemption is provided for many buildings.

The careful balance struck between the rights of individuals with disabilities and the legitimate interests of business is shown in the various phase-in provisions in the ADA. For example, the employment provisions take effect 2 years from today for employers of 25 or more employees. Four years from today that coverage will be extended to employers with 15-24 employees. These phase-in periods and effective dates will permit adequate time for businesses to become acquainted with the ADA's requirements and to take the necessary steps to achieve compliance.

The ADA recognizes the necessity of educating the public about its rights and responsibilities under the Act. Under the ADA, the Attorney General will oversee Government-wide technical assistance activities. The Department of Justice will consult with the Architectural and Transportation Barriers Compliance Board, the Equal Employment Opportunity Commission, the Department of Transportation, the Federal Communications Commission, the National Council on Disability, and the President's Committee on Employment of People with Disabilities, among others, in the effort. We will involve trade associations, advocacy groups, and other similar organizations that have existing lines of communications with covered entities and persons with disabilities. The participation of these organizations is a key element in assuring the success of the technical assistance effort.

In signing this landmark bill, I pledge the full support of my Administration for the Americans with Disabilities Act. It is a great honor to preside over the implementation of the responsibilities conferred on the executive branch by this Act. I pledge that we will fulfill those responsibilities efficiently and vigorously.

The Americans with Disabilities Act presents us all with an historic opportunity. It signals the end to the unjustified segregation and exclusion of persons with disabilities from the mainstream of American life. As the Declaration of Independence has been a beacon for people all over the world seeking freedom, it is my hope that the Americans with Disabilities Act will likewise come to be a model for the choices and opportunities of future generations around the world.

George Bush
The White House
July 26, 1990

INTRODUCTION

This Introduction is drawn from
U.S. House of Representatives Report 101-485, Part IV,
dated May 15, 1990

INTRODUCTION

. Some 43,000,000 Americans have one or more physical or mental disabilities, and this number is increasing as the population as a whole is growing older.

Historically, society has tended to isolate and segregate individuals with disabilities, and, despite some improvements, such forms of discrimination against individuals with disabilities continue to be a serious and pervasive social problem.

Discrimination against individuals with disabilities persists in such critical areas as employment, housing, public accommodations, education, transportation, communication, recreation, institutionalization, health services, voting, and access to public services.

Unlike individuals who have experienced discrimination on the basis of race, color, sex, national origin, religion, or age, individuals who have experienced discrimination on the basis of disability have often had no legal recourse to redress such discrimination.

Individuals with disabilities continually encounter various forms of discrimination, including outright intentional exclusion, the discriminatory effects of architectural, transportation, and communication barriers, overprotective rules and policies, failure to make modifications to existing facilities and practices, exclusionary qualification standards and criteria, segregation, and relegation to lesser services, programs, activities, benefits, jobs, or other opportunities.

Census data, national polls, and other studies have documented that people with disabilities, as a group, occupy an inferior status in our society, and are severely disadvantaged socially, vocationally, economically, and educationally.

Individuals with disabilities are a discrete and insular minority who have been faced with restrictions and limitations, subjected to a history of purposeful unequal treatment, and relegated to a position of political powerlessness in our society, based on characteristics that are beyond the control of such individuals and resulting from stereotypic assumptions not truly indicative of the individual ability of such individuals to participate in, and contribute to, society.

The Nation's proper goals regarding individuals with disabilities are to assure equality of opportunity, full participation, independent living, and economic self-sufficiency for such individuals.

The continuing existence of unfair and unnecessary discrimination and prejudice denies people with disabilities the opportunity to compete on an equal basis and to pursue those opportunities for which our free society is justifiably famous, and costs the United States billions of dollars in unnecessary expenses resulting from dependency and nonproductivity.

It is the purpose of the Americans with Disabilities Act to provide a clear and comprehensive national mandate for the elimination of discrimination against individuals with disabilities; to provide clear, strong, consistent, enforceable standards addressing discrimination against individuals with disabilities; to ensure that the Federal Government plays a central role in enforcing the standards established in this Act on behalf of individuals with disabilities; and to invoke the sweep of congressional authority, including the power to enforce the fourteenth amendment and to regulate commerce, in order to address the major areas of discrimination faced day-to-day by people with disabilities.

DISCRIMINATION ON THE BASIS
OF DISABILITY

*This section on Discrimination on the Basis of Disability
is drawn from
U.S. Senate Report 101-116, dated August 30, 1989*

Discrimination on the Basis of Disability

In General

Testimony presented to the Senate Labor & Human Resources Committee and Subcommittee, two reports by the National Council on Disability ("Toward Independence" (1986) and "On the Threshold of Independence" (1988)), a report by the Civil Rights Commission ("Accommodating the Spectrum of Individual Abilities" (1983)), polls taken by Louis Harris and Associates ("Bringing Disabled Americans into the Mainstream" (March 1986)) and "Employing Disabled Americans" (1987)), a report of the Presidential Commission on the Human Immunodeficiency Virus Epidemic (1988)), and the report by the Task Force on the Rights and Empowerment of Americans with Disabilities all reach the same fundamental conclusions:

(1) Historically, individuals with disabilities have been isolated and subjected to discrimination and such isolation and discrimination is still pervasive in our society;

(2) Discrimination still persists in such critical areas as employment in the private sector, public accommodations, public services, transportation, and telecommunications;

(3) Current Federal and State laws are inadequate to address the discrimination faced by people with disabilities in these critical areas;

(4) People with disabilities as a group occupy an inferior status socially, economically, vocationally, and educationally; and

(5) Discrimination denies people with disabilities the opportunity to compete on an equal basis and costs the

United States, State and local governments, and the private sector billions of dollars in unnecessary expenses resulting from dependency and nonproductivity.

One of the most debilitating forms of discrimination is segregation imposed by others. Timothy Cook of the National Disability Action Center testified:

As Rosa Parks taught us, and as the Supreme Court ruled thirty-five years ago in *Brown v. Board of Education*, segregation "affects one's heart and mind in ways that may never be undone. Separate but equal is inherently unequal."

Discrimination also includes exclusion, or denial of benefits, services, or other opportunities that are as effective and meaningful as those provided to others.

Discrimination results from actions or inactions that discriminate by effect as well as by intent or design. Discrimination also includes harms resulting from the construction of transportation, architectural, and communication barriers and the adoption or application of standards and criteria and practices and procedures based on thoughtlessness or indifference - of benign neglect.

The testimony presented by Judith Heumann, World Institute on Disability, illustrates several of these forms of discrimination:

When I was 5 my mother proudly pushed my wheelchair to our local public school, where I was promptly refused admission because the principal ruled that I was a fire hazard. I was forced to go into home instruction, receiving one hour of education trice a week for 3-1/2 years.

My entrance into mainstream society was blocked by discrimination and segregation. Segregation was not only on an institutional level but also acted as an obstruction to social integration. As a teenager, I could not travel with my friends on the bus because it was not accessible. At my graduation from high school, the principal attempted to prevent me from accepting an award in a ceremony on stage simply because I was in a wheelchair.

When I was 19, the house mother of my college dormitory refused me admission into the dorm because I was in a wheelchair and needed assistance. When I was 21 years old, I was denied an elementary school teaching credential because of "paralysis of both lower extremities sequelae of poliomyelitis." At the time, I did not know what sequelae meant. I went to the dictionary and looked it up and found out that it was "because of." So it was obviously because of my disability that I was discriminated against.

At the age of 25, I was told to leave a plane on my return trip to my job here in the U.S. Senate because I was flying without an attendant. In 1981, an attempt was made to forceably remove me and another disabled friend from an auction house because we were "disgusting to look at." In 1983, a manager at a movie theater attempted to keep my disabled friend and myself out of his theater because we could not transfer out of our wheelchairs.

Discrimination also includes harms affecting individuals with a history of disability, and those regarded by others as having a disability as well as persons associated with such individuals that are based on false presumptions, generalizations, misperceptions, patronizing attitudes, ignorance, irrational fears, and pernicious mythologies.

Discrimination also includes the effects a person's disability may have on others. For example, in March, 1988 the Washington Post reported the story of a New Jersey zoo keeper who refused to admit children with Down's Syndrome because he feared they would upset the chimpanzees. The Supreme Court in *Alexander v. Choate* (1985) cited as an example of improper discrimination on the basis of handicap a case in which "a court ruled that a cerebral palsied child, who was not a physical threat and was academically competitive, should be excluded from public school, because his teacher claimed his physical appearance 'produced a nauseating effect' on his classmates." The Supreme Court in *School Board of Nassau County v. Arline* (1987) cited remarks of Senator Mondale describing a case in which a woman "crippled by arthritis" was denied a job *not* because she could not do the work but because "college trustees [thought] 'normal students shouldn't see her.'"

The Committee heard testimony about a woman from Kentucky who was fired from the job she had held for a number of years because the employer found out that her son, who had become ill with AIDS, had moved into her house so she could care for him. The Committee also heard testimony about former cancer victims, persons with epilepsy, a person with cerebral palsy, and others who had been subjected to similar types of discrimination.

With respect to the pervasiveness of discrimination in our Nation, the National Council explained:

A major obstacle to achieving the societal goals of equal opportunity and full participation of individuals with disabilities is the problem of discrimination. The severity and pervasiveness of discrimination against people with disabilities is well documented.

The U.S. Commission on Civil Rights recently concluded that:

Despite some improvements [discrimination] persists in such critical areas as education, employment, institutionalization, medical treatment, involuntary sterilization, architectural barriers, and transportation.

The Commission further observed that "discriminatory treatment of handicapped persons can occur in almost every aspect of their lives."

The Lou Harris polls found that:

By almost any definition, Americans with disabilities are uniquely underprivileged and disadvantaged. They are much poorer, much less well educated and have much less social life, have fewer amenities and have a lower level of self-satisfaction than other Americans.

Admiral James Watkins, former chairperson of the President's Commission on the Human Immunodeficiency Virus Epidemic, testified that after 45 days of public hearings and site visits, the Commission concluded that discrimination against individuals with HIV infection is widespread and has serious repercussions for both the individual who experiences it and for this Nation's efforts to control the epidemic. The Report concludes:

as long as discrimination occurs, and no strong national policy with rapid and effective remedies against discrim-

ination is established, individuals who are infected with
HIV will be reluctant to come forward for testing, counseling, and care. This fear of potential discrimination
will undermine our efforts to contain the HIV epidemic
and will leave HIV-infected individuals isolated and
alone.

Justin Dart, the chairperson of the Task Force on the
Rights and Empowerment of Americans with Disabilities,
testified that after 63 public forums held in every state,
there is overwhelming evidence that:

Although America has recorded great progress in the
area of disability during the past few decades, our society is still infected by the ancient, now almost subcon-
scious assumption that people with disabilities are less
than fully human and therefore are not fully eligible for
the opportunities, services, and support systems which
are available to other people as a matter of right. The
result is massive, society-wide discrimination.

The U.S. Attorney General, Dick Thornburgh, on behalf of
President Bush, testified that:

Despite the best efforts of all levels of government and
the private sector and the tireless efforts of concerned
citizens and advocates everywhere, many persons with
disabilities in this Nation still lead their lives in an intol-
erable state of isolation and dependence.

Employment

Individuals with disabilities experience staggering levels of
unemployment and poverty. According to a recent Lou
Harris poll not working is perhaps the truest definition of

what it means to be disabled in America. Two-thirds of all disabled Americans between the age of 16 and 64 are not working at all; yet, a large majority of those not working say that they want to work. Sixty-six percent of working-age disabled persons, who are not working, say that they would like to have a job. Translated into absolute terms, this means that about 8.2 million people with disabilities want to work but cannot find a job.

Forty percent of all adults with disabilities did not finish high school - three times more than non-disabled individuals. In 1984, fifty percent of all adults with disabilities had household incomes of $15,000 or less. Among non-disabled persons, only twenty-five percent had household incomes in this wage bracket.

President Bush has stated: "The statistics consistently demonstrate that disabled people are the poorest, least educated and largest minority in America."

According to the Lou Harris poll, the majority of those individuals with disabilities not working and out of the labor force, must depend on insurance payments or government benefits for support. Eighty-two percent of people with disabilities said they would give up their government benefits in favor of a full-time job.

Lou Harris' poll also found that large majorities of top managers (72 percent), equal opportunity officers (76 percent), and department heads/line managers (80 percent) believe that individuals with disabilities often encounter job discrimination from employers and that discrimination by employers remains an inexcusable barrier to increased employment of disabled people.

According to testimony presented to the Committee by Arlene Mayerson of the Disabilities Rights Education and Defense Fund, the major categories of job discrimination faced by people with disabilities include: use of standards and criteria that have the effect of denying opportunities; failure to provide or make available reasonable accommodations; refusal to hire based on presumptions, stereotypes and myths about job performance, safety, insurance costs, absenteeism, and acceptance by co-workers; placement into dead-end jobs; under-employment and lack of promotion opportunities; and use of application forms and other pre-employment inquiries that inquire about the existence of a disability rather than about the ability to perform the essential functions of a job.

Several witnesses also explained that title I of the ADA (employment discrimination) is modeled after regulations implementing the Rehabilitation Act of 1973, which prohibits discrimination by recipients of Federal assistance and requires affirmative action by Federal contractors and that compliance with these laws has been "no big deal."

Harold Russell, the chairperson of the President's Committee on Employment of People with Disabilities, testified that for a majority of employees, for example, no reasonable accommodation is required; for many others the costs can be less than $50. According to the President's Committee which operates the Job Accommodation Network, typical accommodations provided for under $50 include:

A timer costing $26.95 with an indicator light allowed a medical technician who was deaf to perform the laboratory tests required for her job;

A receptionist who was visually impaired was provided with a light probe, costing $45, which allowed her to determine which lines on a telephone were ringing, on hold, or in use of her company;

Obtaining a headset for a phone costing $49.95 allowed an insurance salesperson with cerebral palsy to write while talking.

Witnesses also explained that there will also be a need for more expensive accommodations, including readers for blind persons and interpreters for deaf persons. But even costs for these accommodations are frequently exaggerated. Dr. I. King Jordan, President of Gallaudet University, explained to the Committee:

Often, interpreters can be hired to do other things as well as interpret - administrative secretaries or professional staff, even, who interpret on an only-as-needed basis. Most of the time, people who are hired who are deaf function without an interpreter except when they are in a meeting or except when they are attending a workshop or except when there is a very essential need for one-to-one communication. But, I think it needs to be made clear to people that the accommodations are not nearly as large as some people would lead us to believe.

In sum, testimony indicates that the provision of all types of reasonable accommodations is essential to accomplishing the critical goal of this legislation - to allow individuals with disabilities to be part of the economic mainstream of our society.

Public Accommodations

Based on testimony presented at the hearings and recent national surveys and reports, it is clear that an overwhelming majority of individuals with disabilities lead isolated lives and do not frequent places of public accommodation.

The National Council on Disability summarized the findings of a recent Lou Harris poll:

> The survey results dealing with social life and leisure experiences paint a sobering picture of an isolated and secluded population of individuals with disabilities. The large majority of people with disabilities do not go to movies, do not go to the theater, do not go to see musical performances, and do not go to sports events. A substantial minority of persons with disabilities never go to a restaurant, never go to a grocery store, and never go to a church or synagogue. The extent of non-participation of individuals with disabilities in social and recreational activities is alarming.

Several witnesses addressed the obvious question "Why don't people with disabilities frequent places of public accommodations and stores as often as other Americans?" Three major reasons were given by witnesses. The first reason is that people with disabilities do not feel that they are welcome and can participate safely in such places. The second reason is fear and self-consciousness about their disability stemming from degrading experiences they or their friends with disabilities have experienced. The third reason is architectural, communication, and transportation barriers.

Former Senator Lowell Weicker testified that people with disabilities spend a lifetime "overcoming not what God wrought but what man imposed by custom and law."

Witnesses also testified about the need to define places of public accommodations to include all places open to the public, not simply restaurants, hotels, and places of entertainment (which are the types of establishments covered by title II of the Civil Rights Act of 1964) because discrimination against people with disabilities is not limited to specific categories of public accommodations. The Attorney General stated that we must bring Americans with disabilities into the mainstream of society "in other words, full participation in and access to all aspects of society."

Robert Burgdorf, Jr., currently a Professor of Law at the District of Columbia School of Law, testifying on behalf of the National Easter Seal Society, stated:

> it makes no sense to bar discrimination against people with disabilities in theaters, restaurants, or places of entertainment but not in regard to such important things as doctors' offices. It makes no sense for a law to say that people with disabilities cannot be discriminated against if they want to buy a pastrami sandwich at the local deli but that they can be discriminated against next door at the pharmacy where they need to fill a prescription. There is no sense to that distinction.

Witnesses identified the major areas of discrimination that need to be addressed. The first is lack of physical access to facilities. Witnesses recognized that it is probably not feasible to require that existing facilities be completely retrofitted to be made accessible. However, it is appropriate to require modest changes. Ron Mace, an architect, described numerous inexpensive changes that could be made to make a facility accessible, including installing a permanent or portable ramp over an entrance step; installing offset hinges to widen a doorway; relocating a vending machine to clear an accessible path; and installing signage to indicate accessible routes and features within facilities.

Several witnesses also recognized that when renovations are made that affect or could affect usability, the renovations should enhance accessibility and that newly constructed buildings should be fully accessible because the additional costs for making new facilities accessible are often "negligible." According to Ron Mace, there is absolutely no reason why new buildings constructed in America cannot be barrier-free since additional cost is not the factor. He testified that the problem is that "there is right now no training provided for designers in our country on how to design for children, older people and disabled people."

Additional areas of discrimination that witnesses identified include: the imposition or application of standards or criteria that limit or exclude people with disabilities; the failure to make reasonable modifications in policies to allow participation, and a failure to provide auxiliary aids and services.

For example, Greg Hlibok, student President of Gallaudet University, testified about the need for places of public accommodations to take steps to enhance safety for persons with hearing impairments. Laura Oftedahl of the Columbia Lighthouse for the Blind testified about the lack of access and unnecessary dangers visually impaired people face because of lack of simple, inexpensive auxiliary aids.

Public Services

Currently, Federal law prohibits recipients of Federal assistance from discriminating against individuals with disabilities. Many agencies of State and local government receive Federal aid and thus are currently prohibited from engaging in discrimination on the basis of disability. Witnesses testified about the inequity of limiting protection based on the receipt of Federal funding. For example, Neil Hartigan, the Attorney General from Illinois, testified that:

> Under the current Federal law, the Rehabilitation Act's nondiscrimination requirements are tied to the receipt of Federal financial assistance. Unfortunately, what this translates to is total confusion for the disabled community and the inability to expect consistent treatment. Where there is no state law prohibiting discriminatory practices, two programs that are exactly alike, except for funding sources, can treat people with disabilities completely differently than others who don't have disabilities.

Mr. Hartigan also focused on the need to ensure access to polling places: "You cannot exercise one of your most basic rights as an American if the polling places are not accessible." The Committee heard about people with disabilities who were forced to vote by absentee ballot before key debates by the candidates were held.

Dr. Mary Lynn Fletcher of Disability Services testified that access to all public services is particularly critical in rural areas, because State and local government activities are frequently the major activities in such small towns. Since Federal aid frequently does not reach small rural towns, current law thus does not protect people with disabilities in such areas from discrimination.

Transportation

Transportation is the linchpin which enables people with disabilities to be integrated and mainstreamed into society. Timothy Cook of the National Disability Action Center testified that "access to transportation is the key to opening up education, employment, recreation; and other provisions of the [ADA] are meaningless unless we put together an accessible public transportation system in this country." The National Council on Disability has declared that "accessible transportation is a critical component of a national policy that promotes the self-reliance and self-sufficiency of people with disabilities."

Harold Russell, testifying for the President's Committee on Employment of People with Disabilities, made the same point when he stated:

> To have less than adequate accessible public transportation services for an individual who is protected from discrimination in employment, or who has received other numerous federally funded services, is analogous to throwing an 11-foot rope to a drowning man 20 feet offshore and then proclaiming you are going more than halfway.

Witnesses also testified about the need to pursue a multimodal approach to ensuring access for people with disabilities which provides that all new buses used for fixed routes are accessible and paratransit is made available for those who cannot use the fixed route accessible buses.

For some people with disabilities who lead or would like to lead spontaneous, independent lives integrated into the community, paratransit is often inadequate or inappropriate for the following reasons, among others: the need to make reservations in advance often conflicts with one's work schedule or interests in going out to restaurants and the like; the cost of rides when used frequently is often exorbitant; limitations on time of day and the number of days that the paratransit operates; waiting time; restrictions on use by guests and nondisabled companions who are excluded from accompanying the person with a disability; the expense to the public agency; and restrictions on eligibility placed on use by social service agencies.

However, witnesses also stressed that there are some people with disabilities who are so severely disabled that they cannot use accessible mainline transit and thus there is a need to have a paratransit system for these people.

Witnesses also addressed common myths about making mainline buses accessible. Harold Jenkins, the General Manager of the Cambria County Transit Authority in Johnstown, Pennsylvania, testified that his system is 100% accessible and operates without problem, notwithstanding hilly terrain and inclement weather, including snow, flooding, and significant extremes in temperature.

He also explained that when the decision was initially made to make the fleet 100% accessible there was fear and reluctance on the part of the disability community, the drivers, and the general public. That fear and reluctance has now disappeared. Jenkins concluded that mainline access works in his community because of the commitment by everyone to make it work. Thus, there is a need to train and educate top management, drivers, and the general public as well as the disability community.

The Committee also heard and received written testimony that the new generation of lifts are not having the maintenance problems experienced in the past and they can operate in inclement weather. The Architectural Transportation Barriers Compliance Board has reported that currently most problems with lift operation are the direct result of driver error and that lift maintenance is but one facet of a good maintenance program. Thus, transit authorities reporting problems with lifts are generally those that also report problems with general maintenance.

With respect to intercity transportation, the Committee learned about reasonably priced lifts that can be installed on buses which will enable people using wheelchairs to have access to these buses. This is particularly critical in rural areas where these buses are often the only mode of transportation that is available.

Telecommunications

Dr. I. King Jordan, President of Gallaudet University, noted to the Committee that more than 100 years ago Alexander Graham Bell invented the telephone in the hope that he could close the communication gap between deaf and hearing people. According to Dr. Jordan: "Not only did the telephone not help close the gap, but in many ways it widened it and has become one more barrier in the lives of deaf people."

Several witnesses testified about the critical need to establish relay systems which will enable hearing impaired and communication impaired persons who use telecommunication devices for the deaf (TDDs) to make calls to and receive calls from individuals using voice telephones. Dr. Jordan explained:

The simplest task often becomes a major burden when we do not have access to the telephone: the person who wants to call a doctor for an appointment or the person who has to call his boss and tell him he cannot show up for work that day, someone at home who needs to call a plumber to fix a leak, or maybe a theatergoer who wants to make reservations or go to dinner.

Robert Yeager, who operates the Minnesota Relay Service, explained the importance of the relay this way:

As a former relay operator myself, I have seen the difference these services can make in people's lives.   A women calls an ambulance when her husband has a heart attack; someone sets up a job interview and gets a job; a teenager gets their first date.

Dr. Jordan summed up the need for a national relay system by stating:

The phone is a necessity, and it is a necessity for all of us, not just people who can hear.   By requiring nationwide telephone relay service for everyone, it will help deaf people achieve a level of independence in employment and public accommodations that is sought by other parts of the ADA.

Enforcement

Several witnesses emphasized that the rights guaranteed by the ADA are meaningless without effective enforcement provisions.   Illinois Attorney General Neil Hartigan explained that:

The whole trick is to make it more expensive to break the law than it is to keep the law. The vast majority of businesspeople want to keep the law. They just have got a bottom line they have got to meet. They can't have somebody else having an unfair competitive advantage by getting away with a discriminatory practice. That is why we need teeth in the law. That is why we put the penalties in the law and the damages in the law.

Mr. Hartigan explained that the inclusion of penalties and damages is the driving force that facilitates voluntary compliance:

When you don't have the penalties, there [are] no enforcement possibilities. Right now we can have traditional as well as punitive damages. We can have injunctive activity. We have got a range of weapons we can use if we have to use them. But, the fact that you've got it, the fact they know you are serious about it, keeps you from having to use it. We have 3,000 cases where we haven't had to go to court.

Summary

In sum, the unfortunate truth is that individuals with disabilities are a discrete and insular minority who have been faced with restrictions and limitations, subjected to a history of purposeful unequal treatment, and relegated to a position of political powerlessness in our society, based on characteristics that are beyond the control of such individuals and resulting from stereotypic assumptions not truly indicative of the ability of such individuals to participate in and contribute to society.

The Effects of Discrimination on Individuals with Disabilities

Discrimination has many different effects on individuals with disabilities. Arlene Mayerson of the Disabilities Rights Education and Defense Fund testified about the nature of discrimination against people with disabilities:

> The discriminatory nature of policies and practices that exclude and segregate disabled people has been obscured by the unchallenged equation of disability with incapacity and by the gloss of "good intentions." The innate biological and physical "inferiority" of disabled people is considered self-evident. This "self-evident" proposition has served to justify the exclusion and segregation of disabled people from all aspects of life. The social consequences that have attached to being disabled often bear no relationship to the physical or mental limitations imposed by the disability. For example, being paralyzed has meant far more than being unable to walk - it has meant being excluded from public schools, being denied employment opportunities and being deemed an "unfit parent." These injustices coexist with an atmosphere of charity and concern for disabled people.

Dr. I. King Jordan, the President of Gallaudet University, explained that:

> Discrimination occurs in every facet of our lives. There is not a disabled American alive today who has not experienced some form of discrimination. Of course, this has very serious consequences. It destroys healthy self-concepts and slowly erodes the human spirit. Discrimination does not belong in the lives of disabled people.

Judith Heumann of the World Institute on Disability explained that:

> In the past, disability has been a cause of shame. This forced acceptance of second-class citizenship has stripped us as disabled people of pride and dignity. This stigma scars for life.

Discrimination produces fear and reluctance to participate. Robert Burgdorf of the National Easter Seal Society and Harold Jenkins of the Cambria County Transit Authority testified that fear of mistreatment and discrimination and the existence of architectural, transportation, and communication barriers are critical reasons why individuals with disabilities don't participate to the same extent as nondisabled people in public accommodations and transportation.

Dr. Mary Lynn Fletcher testified about the factors that isolate people with disabilities and then explained that when one adds the rural factor on top of everything else it "obliterates the person."

Discrimination results in social isolation and in some cases suicide.

Justin Dart of the Task Force on the Rights & Empowerment of Americans with Disabilities testified before the Committee about how several of his brothers had committed suicide because of their disabilities and about a California woman, a mother, a TV director before becoming disabled who said to him:

> We can go just so long constantly reaching dead ends. I am broke, degraded, and angry, have attempted suicide three times. I know hundreds. Most of us try, but

which way and where can we go? What and who can we be? If I were understood, I would have something to live for.

The Effects of Discrimination on Society

The Committee also heard testimony and reviewed reports concluding that discrimination results in dependency on social welfare programs that cost the taxpayers unnecessary billions of dollars each year. Sandy Parrino, the chairperson of the National Council on Disability, testified that discrimination places people with disabilities in chains that:

bind many of the 36 million people into a bondage of unjust, unwanted dependency on families, charity, and social welfare. Dependency that is a major and totally unnecessary contributor to public deficits and private expenditures.

She added that:

it is contrary to sound principles of fiscal responsibility to spend billions of Federal tax dollars to relegate people with disabilities to positions of dependency upon public support.

President Bush has stated:

On the cost side, the National Council on the Handicapped states that current spending on disability benefits and programs exceeds $60 billion annually. Excluding the millions of disabled who want to work from the employment ranks costs society literally billions of dollars annually in support payments and lost income tax revenues.

Attorney General Thornburgh added that:

> We must recognize that passing comprehensive civil
> rights legislation protecting persons with disabilities will
> have direct and tangible benefits for our country. Cer-
> tainly, the elimination of employment discrimination
> and the mainstreaming of persons with disabilities will
> result in more persons with disabilities working, in in-
> creased earnings, in less dependence on the Social Securi-
> ty system for financial support, in increased spending on
> consumer goods, and increased tax revenues.

Justin Dart testified that it is discrimination and segregation that are preventing persons with disabilities from becoming self-reliant:

> and that are driving us inevitably towards an economic
> and moral disaster of giant, paternalistic welfare bu-
> reaucracy. We are already paying unaffordable and rap-
> idly escalating billions in public and private funds to
> maintain ever-increasing millions of potentially produc-
> tive Americans in unjust, unwanted dependency.

Thus, discrimination makes people with disabilities depend-
ent on social welfare programs rather than allowing them
to be taxpayers and consumers.

Discrimination also deprives our Nation of a valuable
source of labor in a period of labor shortages in certain
jobs.

President Bush has stated:

The United States is now beginning to face labor shortages
as the baby boomers move through the work force.

The disabled offer a pool of talented workers whom we simply cannot afford to ignore, especially in connection with the high tech growth industries of the future.

Jay Rochlin, the executive director of the President's Committee on Employment of People with Disabilities, has stated:

The demographics have given us an unprecedented 20 year window of opportunity. Employers will be desperate to find qualified employees. Of necessity, they will have to look beyond their traditional sources of personnel and work to attract minorities, women, and others for a new workforce. Our challenge is to insure that the largest minority, people with disabilities, is included.

Discrimination also negates the billions of dollars we invest each year to educate our children and youth with disabilities and train and rehabilitate adults with disabilities. Dr. I. King Jordan testified that:

We must stop sending disabled youth conflicting signals. America makes substantial investments in the education and development of these young people, then we deny them the opportunity to succeed and to graduate into a world that treats them with dignity and respect.

Sylvia Piper, a parent of a child with developmental disabilities testified that:

We have invested in Dan's future. And the Ankeny Public School District has made an investment in Dan's future. Are we going to allow this investment of time, energy, and dollars, not to mention Dan's ability and quality of life, to cease when he reaches 21?

Attorney General Richard Thornburgh made the same point in his testimony:

The continued maintenance of these barriers imposes staggering economic and social costs and inhibits our sincere and substantial Federal commitment to the education, rehabilitation, and employment of persons with disabilities. The elimination of these barriers will enable society to benefit from the skills and talents of per sons with disabilities and will enable persons with disabilities to lead more productive lives.

Current Federal and State Laws

State laws are inadequate to address the pervasive problems of discrimination that people with disabilities are facing. As Neil Hartigan testified:

This is a crucial area where the Federal Government can act to establish uniform minimum requirements for accessibility.

Admiral Watkins of the President's Commission on the Human Immunodeficiency Virus Epidemic testified that:

My predecessor [Sandy Parrino] here this morning said enough time has, in my opinion, been given to the States to legislate what is right. Too many States, for whatever reason, still perpetuate confusion. It is time for Federal action.

According to Harold Russell:

The fifty State Governors' Committees, with whom the President's Committee works, report that existing State laws do not adequately counter such acts of discrimination.

Current Federal law is also inadequate. Currently, Federal anti-discrimination laws only address discrimination by Federal agencies and recipients of Federal financial assistance. Last year, Congress amended the Fair Housing Act to prohibit discrimination against people with disabilities. However, there are still no protections against discrimination by employers in the private sector, by places of public accommodation, by State and local government agencies that do not receive Federal aid, and with respect to the provision of telecommunication services. With respect to the provision of accessible transportation services, there are still misinterpretations by executive agencies and some courts regarding transportation by public entities and lack of protection against private transportation companies.

The need to enact omnibus civil rights legislation for individuals with disabilities was one of the major recommendations of the National Council on Disability in its two most recent reports to Congress. In fact S. 2345, the Americans With Disabilities Act of 1988, introduced during the 100th Congress, was developed by the Council.

The need for omnibus civil rights legislation was also one of the major recommendations of the Presidential Commission on the HIV Epidemic:

Comprehensive Federal anti-discrimination legislation, which prohibits discrimination against persons with disabilities in the public and private sectors, including employment, housing, public accommodations and participation in government programs should be enacted. All persons with symptomatic or asymptomatic HIV infection should be clearly included as persons with disabilities who are covered by the anti-discrimination protections of this legislation.

Attorney General Thornburgh, on behalf of President Bush, also testified about the importance of enacting comprehensive civil rights legislation for people with disabilities:

The Committee is to be commended for its efforts in drafting S. 933. One of its most impressive strengths is its comprehensive character. Over the last 20 years, civil rights laws protecting disabled persons have been enacted in piecemeal fashion. Thus, existing Federal laws are like a patchwork quilt in need of repair. There are holes in the fabric, serious gaps in coverage that leave persons with disabilities without adequate civil rights protections.

Vision for the Future

Many of the witnesses described the vision of the Americans With Disabilities Act.

Sandy Parrino of the National Council on the Handicapped testified that:

Martin Luther King had a dream. We have a vision. Dr. King dreamed of an America "where a person is judged not by the color of his skin, but by the content of his character." ADA's vision is of an America where persons are judged by their abilities and not on the basis of their disabilities.

Tony Coelho, Majority Whip of the House of Representatives, shared the following observation with the Committee:

> While the charity model once represented a step forward in the treatment of persons with handicaps, in today's society it is irrelevant, inappropriate and a great disservice. Our model must change. Disabled people are sometimes impatient, and sometimes angry, but for good reason - they are fed up with discrimination and exclusion, tired of denial, and are eager to seize the challenges and opportunities as quickly as the rest of us.

Dr. Jordan testified that the ADA is necessary to demonstrate that disabled people:

> Can have the same aspirations and dreams as other American citizens. Disabled persons know that their dreams can be fulfilled.

Dr. Jordan also testified that passage of ADA:

> Will tell disabled Americans that they are indeed equal to other Americans and that discrimination toward disabled persons will no longer be tolerated in our country. It will also make a powerful statement to the world that America is true to its ideals. That is the full measure of the American dream.

Perry Tillman, a Vietnam veteran, testified that:

> I did my job when I was called on by my country. Now it is your job and the job of everyone in Congress to make sure that when I lost the use of my legs I didn't lose my ability to achieve my dreams. Myself and other

veterans before me fought for freedom for all Americans. But when I came home and found out that what I fought for applied to everyone but me and other handicapped people, I couldn't stop fighting. I have fought since my injury in Vietnam to regain my rightful place in society. I ask that you now join me in ending this fight and give quick and favorable consideration to the ADA in order to allow all Americans, disabled or not, to take part equally in American life.

Conclusion

In conclusion, the Committee found that there is a compelling need to provide a clear and comprehensive national mandate for the elimination of discrimination against individuals with disabilities and for the integration of persons with disabilities into the economic and social mainstream of American life. Further, there is a need to provide clear, strong, consistent, enforceable standards addressing discrimination against individuals with disabilities. Finally, there is a need to ensure that the Federal Government plays a central role in enforcing these standards on behalf of individuals with disabilities.

QUESTIONS AND ANSWERS

This Questions and Answers section is drawn from:

The Americans with Disabilities Act: Questions and Answers
published by the
U.S. Equal Employment Opportunity Commission and the
U.S. Department of Justice, Civil Rights Division

and

The Americans with Disabilities Act:
Your Responsibilities as an Employer,
published by the
U.S. Equal Employment Opportunity Commission

QUESTIONS AND ANSWERS

Employment

What employers are covered by the ADA, and when is the coverage effective?

The employment provisions apply to private employers, State and local governments, employment agencies, and labor unions. Employers with 25 or more employees will be covered starting July 26, 1992, when the employment provisions go into effect. Employers with 15 or more employees will be covered two years later, beginning July 26, 1994.

What practices and activities are covered by the employment nondiscrimination requirements?

The ADA prohibits discrimination in all employment practices, including job application procedures, hiring, firing, advancement, compensation, training, and other terms, conditions, and privileges of employment. It applies to recruitment, advertising, tenure, layoff, leave, fringe benefits, and all other employment-related activities.

Who is protected against employment discrimination?

Employment discrimination is prohibited against "qualified individuals with disabilities." Persons discriminated against because they have a known association or relationship with a disabled individual also are protected. The ADA defines an "individual with a disability" as a person who has a physical or mental impairment that substantially limits one or more major life activities, a record of such an impairment, or is regarded as having such an impairment.

The first part of the definition makes clear that the ADA applies to persons who have substantial, as distinct from minor, impairments, and that these must be impairments that limit major life activities such as seeing, hearing, speaking, walking, breathing, performing manual tasks, learning, caring for oneself, and working. An individual with epilepsy, paralysis, a substantial hearing or visual impairment, mental retardation, or a learning disability would be covered, but an individual with a minor, nonchronic condition of short duration, such as a sprain, infection, or broken limb, generally would not be covered.

The second part of the definition would include, for example, a person with a history of cancer that is currently in remission or a person with a history of mental illness.

The third part of the definition protects individuals who are regarded and treated as though they have a substantially limiting disability, even though they may not have such an impairment. For example, this provision would protect a severely disfigured qualified individual from being denied employment because an employer feared the "negative reactions" of others.

Who is a "qualified individual with a disability?"

A qualified individual with a disability is a person who meets legitimate skill, experience, education, or other requirements of an employment position that he or she holds or seeks, and who can perform the "essential functions" of the position with or without reasonable accommodation. Requiring the ability to perform "essential" functions assures that an individual will not be considered unqualified simply because of inability to perform marginal or incidental job functions. If the individual is qualified to perform essential job functions except for limitations caused by a disability, the employer must consider whether the individual could perform these functions with a reasonable accommodation. If a written job description has been prepared in advance of advertising or interviewing applicants for a job, this will be considered as evidence, although not necessarily conclusive evidence, of the essential functions of the job.

How are essential functions determined?

Essential functions are the basic job duties that an employee must be able to perform, with or without reasonable accommodation. Each job should be carefully examined to determine which functions or tasks are essential to performance. (This is particularly important before taking an employment action such as recruiting, advertising, hiring, promoting or firing).

Factors to consider in determining if a function is essential include:

whether the reason the position exists is to perform that function,

the number of other employees available to perform the function or among whom the performance of the function can be distributed, and

the degree of expertise or skill required to perform the function.

An employer's judgment as to which functions are essential, and a written job description prepared before advertising or interviewing for a job will be considered by EEOC

as evidence of essential functions. Other kinds of evidence
that EEOC will consider include:

actual work experience of present or past employees in
the job,

time spent performing a function,

consequences of not requiring that an employee perform
a function, and

terms of a collective bargaining agreement.

Does an employer have to give preference to a qualified applicant with a disability over other applicants?

No. An employer is free to select the most qualified applicant available and to make decisions based on reasons unrelated to the existence or consequence of a disability. For example, if two persons apply for a job opening as a typist, one a person with a disability who accurately types 50 words per minute, the other a person without a disability who accurately types 75 words per minute, the employer may hire the applicant with the higher typing speed, if typing speed is needed for successful performance of the job.

What is "reasonable accommodation"?

Reasonable accommodation is any modification or adjustment to a job or the work environment that will enable a qualified applicant or employee with a disability to participate in the application process or to perform essential job functions. Reasonable accommodation also includes adjustments to assure that a qualified individual with a disability has the same rights and privileges in employment as nondisabled employees.

What kinds of actions are required to reasonably accommodate applicants and employees?

Examples of reasonable accommodation include making existing facilities used by employees readily accessible to and usable by an individual with a disability; restructuring a job; modifying work schedules; acquiring or modifying equipment; providing qualified readers or interpreters; or appropriately modifying examinations, training, or other programs. Reasonable accommodation also may include reassigning a current employee to a vacant position for which the individual is qualified, if the person becomes disabled and is unable to do the original job. However, there is no obligation to find a position for an applicant who is not qualified for the position sought. Employers are not required to lower quality or quantity standards in order to make an accommodation, nor are they obligated to provide personal use items such as glasses or hearing aids.

The decision as to the appropriate accommodation must be based on the particular facts of each case. In selecting the particular type of reasonable accommodation to provide, the principal test is that of effectiveness, i.e., whether the accommodation will enable the person with a disability to do the job in question.

Must employers be familiar with the many diverse types of disabilities to know whether or how to make a reasonable accommodation?

No. An employer is only required to accommodate a "known" disability of a qualified applicant or employee.

The requirement generally will be triggered by a request from an individual with a disability, who frequently can suggest an appropriate accommodation. Accommodations must be made on an individual basis, because the nature and extent of a disabling condition and the requirements of the job will vary in each case. If the individual does not request an accommodation, the employer is not obligated to provide one. If a disabled person requests, but cannot suggest, an appropriate accommodation, the employer and the individual should work together to identify one. There are also many public and private resources that can provide assistance without cost.

What are the limitations on the obligation to make a reasonable accommodation?

The disabled individual requiring the accommodation must be otherwise qualified, and the disability must be known to the employer. In addition, an employer is not required to make an accommodation if it would impose an "undue hardship" on the operation of the employer's business. "Undue hardship" is defined as "an action requiring significant difficulty or expense" when considered in light of a number of factors. These factors include the nature and cost of the accommodation in relation to the size, resources, nature, and structure of the employer's operation. Where the facility making the accommodation is part of a larger entity, the structure and overall resources of the larger organization would be considered, as well as the financial and administrative relationship of the facility to the larger organization. In general, a larger employer would be expected to make accommodations requiring greater effort or expense than would be required of a smaller employer.

Must an employer modify existing facilities to make them accessible?

An employer may be required to modify facilities to enable an individual to perform essential job functions and to have equal opportunity to participate in other employment-related activities. For example, if an employee lounge is located in a place inaccessible to a person using a wheelchair, the lounge might be modified or relocated, or comparable facilities might be provided in a location that would enable the individual to take a break with co-workers.

May an employer inquire as to whether a prospective employee is disabled?

An employer may not make a pre-employment inquiry on an application form or in an interview as to whether, or to what extent, an individual is disabled. The employer may ask a job applicant whether he or she can perform particular job functions. If the applicant has a disability known to the employer, the employer may ask how he or she can perform job functions that the employer considers difficult or impossible to perform because of the disability, and whether an accommodation would be needed. A job offer may be conditioned on the results of a medical examination, provided that the examination is required for all entering employees in the same job category regardless of disability, and that information obtained is handled according to confidentiality requirements specified in the Act. After an employee enters on duty, all medical examinations and inquiries must be job related and necessary for the conduct of the employer's business. These provisions of the law are intended to prevent the employer from basing hiring and employment decisions on unfounded assumptions about the effects of a disability.

One of my employees is a diabetic, but takes insulin daily to control his diabetes. As a result, the diabetes has no significant impact on his employment. Is he protected by the ADA?

Yes. The determination as to whether a person has a disability under the ADA is made without regard to mitigating measures, such as medications, auxiliary aids and reasonable accommodations. If an individual has an impairment that substantially limits a major life activity, she is protected under the ADA, regardless of the fact that the disease or condition or its effects may be corrected or controlled.

One of my employees has a broken arm that will heal but is temporarily unable to perform the essential functions of his job as a mechanic. Is this employee protected by the ADA?

No. Although this employee does have an impairment, it does not substantially limit a major life activity if it is of limited duration and will have no long term effect.

When must I consider reassigning an employee with a disability to another job as a reasonable accommodation?

When an employee with a disability is unable to perform her present job even with the provision of a reasonable accommodation, you must consider reassigning the employee to an existing position that she can perform with or without a reasonable accommodation. The requirement to consider reassignment applies only to employees and not to applicants. You are not required to create a position or to bump another employee in order to create a vacancy. Nor are you required to promote an employee with a disability to a higher level position.

What if an applicant or employee refuses to accept an accommodation that I offer?

The ADA provides that an employer cannot require a qualified individual with a disability to accept an accommodation that is neither requested nor needed by the individual. However, if a necessary reasonable accommodation is refused, the individual may be considered not qualified.

If our business has a fitness room for its employees, must it be accessible to employees with disabilities?

Yes. Under the ADA, workers with disabilities must have equal access to all benefits and privileges of employment that are available to similarly situated employees without disabilities. The duty to provide reasonable accommodation applies to all non-work facilities provided or maintained by you for your employees. This includes cafeterias, lounges, auditoriums, company-provided transportation and counseling services. If making an existing facility accessible would be an undue hardship, you must provide a comparable facility that will enable a person with a disability to enjoy benefits and privileges of employment similar to those enjoyed by other employees, unless this would be an undue hardship.

If I contract for a consulting firm to develop a training course for my employees, and the firm arranges for the course to be held at a hotel that is inaccessible to one of my employees, am I liable under the ADA?

Yes. An employer may not do through a contractual or other relationship what it is prohibited from doing directly. You would be required to provide a location that is readily accessible to, and usable by your employee with a disability unless to do so would create an undue hardship.

Am I required to provide additional insurance for employees with disabilities?

No. The ADA only requires that you provide an employee with a disability equal access to whatever health insurance coverage you provide to other employees. For example, if your health insurance coverage for certain treatments is limited to a specified number per year, and an employee, because of a disability, needs more than the specified number, the ADA does not require that you provide additional coverage to meet that employee's health insurance needs. The ADA also does not require changes in insurance plans that exclude or limit coverage for pre-existing conditions.

Does the ADA take safety issues into account?

Yes. The ADA permits employers to establish qualification standards that will exclude individuals who pose a direct threat - i.e., a significant risk - to the health and safety of the individual or of others, if that risk cannot be lowered to an acceptable level by reasonable accommodation. However, an employer may not simply assume that a threat exists; the employer must establish through objective, medically supportable methods that there is genuine risk that substantial harm could occur in the workplace. By requiring employers to make individualized judgments based on reliable medical or other objective evidence rather than on generalizations, ignorance, fear, patronizing attitudes, or stereotypes, the ADA recognizes the need to balance the interests of people with disabilities against the legitimate interests of employers in maintaining a safe workplace.

Can an employer refuse to hire an applicant or fire a current employee who is illegally using drugs?

Yes. Individuals who currently engage in the illegal use of drugs are specifically excluded from the definition of a "qualified individual with a disability" protected by the ADA when an action is taken on the basis of their drug use.

Is testing for illegal drugs permissible under the ADA?

Yes. A test for illegal drugs is not considered a medical examination under the ADA; therefore, employers may conduct such testing of applicants or employees and make employment decisions based on the results. The ADA does not encourage, prohibit, or authorize drug tests.

Are people with AIDS covered by the ADA?

Yes. The legislative history indicates that Congress intended the ADA to protect persons with AIDS and HIV disease from discrimination.

How does the ADA recognize public health concerns?

No provision in the ADA is intended to supplant the role of public health authorities in protecting the community from legitimate health threats. The ADA recognizes the need to strike a balance between the right of a disabled person to be free from discrimination based on unfounded fear and the right of the public to be protected.

What is discrimination based on "relationship or association"?

The ADA prohibits discrimination based on relationship or association in order to protect individuals from actions based on unfounded assumptions that their relationship to a person with a disability would affect their job performance, and from actions caused by bias or misinformation concerning certain disabilities. For example, this provision would protect a person with a disabled spouse from being denied employment because of an employer's unfounded assumption that the applicant would use excessive leave to care for the spouse. It also would protect an individual who does volunteer work for people with AIDS from a discriminatory employment action motivated by that relationship or association.

Will the ADA increase litigation burdens on employers?

Some litigation is inevitable. However, employers who use the period prior to the effective date of employment coverage to adjust their policies and practices to conform to ADA requirements will be much less likely to have serious litigation concerns. In drafting the ADA, Congress relied heavily on the language of the Rehabilitation Act of 1973 and its implementing regulations. There is already an extensive body of law interpreting the requirements of that Act to which employers can turn for guidance on their ADA obligations. The Equal Employment Opportunity Commission has issued specific regulatory guidance, and published a technical assistance manual with guidance on how to comply, and provide other assistance to help employers meet ADA requirements. Equal employment opportunity for people with disabilities will be achieved most quickly and effectively through widespread voluntary compliance with the law, rather than through reliance on litigation to enforce compliance.

Does the ADA require that I post a notice explaining its requirements?

The ADA requires that you post a notice in an accessible format to applicants, employees and members of labor organizations, describing the provisions of the Act. EEOC will provide employers with a poster summarizing these and other federal legal requirements for nondiscrimination. EEOC will also provide guidance on making this information available in accessible formats for people with disabilities.

How will the employment provisions be enforced?

The employment provisions of the ADA will be enforced under the same procedures now applicable to race, sex, national origin, and religious discrimination under title VII of the Civil Rights Act of 1964. Complaints regarding actions that occur after July 26, 1992, may be filed with the Equal Employment Opportunity Commission or designated State human rights agencies. Available remedies will include hiring, reinstatement, back pay, and court orders to stop discrimination.

How will EEOC help employers who want to comply with the ADA?

The Commission believes that employers want to comply with the ADA, and that if they are given sufficient information on how to comply, they will do so voluntarily.

Accordingly, the Commission will conduct an active technical assistance program to promote voluntary compliance
with the ADA. This program will be designed to help employers understand their responsibilities and assist people
with disabilities to understand their rights and the law.

EEOC has published a Technical Assistance Manual, providing practical application of legal requirements to specific employment activities, with a directory of resources to
aid compliance. EEOC will publish other educational materials, provide training on the law for employers and for
people with disabilities, and participate in meetings and
training programs of other organizations. EEOC staff also
will respond to individual requests for information and assistance. The Commission's technical assistance program
will be separate and distinct from its enforcement responsibilities. Employers who seek information or assistance
from the Commission will not be subject to any enforcement action because of such inquiries.

The Commission also recognizes that differences and disputes about the ADA requirements may arise between employers and people with disabilities as a result of misunder-
standings. Such disputes frequently can be resolved more
effectively through informal negotiation or mediation
procedures, rather than through the formal enforcement
process of the ADA. Accordingly, EEOC will encourage
efforts to settle such differences through alternative dispute resolution, providing that such efforts do not deprive
any individual of legal rights provided by the statute.

Public Accommodations

What are public accommodations?

Public accommodations are private entities that affect commerce. The ADA public accommodations requirements extend, therefore, to a wide range of entities, such as restaurants, hotels, theaters, doctors' offices, pharmacies, retail stores, museums, libraries, parks, private schools, and day care centers. Private clubs and religious organizations are exempt from the ADA's requirements for public accommodations.

Will the ADA have any effect on the eligibility criteria used by public accommodations to determine who may receive services?

Yes. If a criterion screens out or tends to screen out individuals with disabilities, it may only be used if necessary for the provision of the services. For instance, it would be a violation for a retail store to have a rule excluding all deaf persons from entering the premises, or for a movie theater to exclude all individuals with cerebral palsy. More subtle forms of discrimination are also prohibited. For example, requiring presentation of a driver's license as the sole acceptable means of identification for purposes of paying by check could constitute discrimination against individuals with vision impairments. This would be true if such individuals are ineligible to receive licenses and the use of an alternative means of identification is feasible.

Does the ADA allow public accommodations to take safety factors into consideration in providing services to individuals with disabilities?

The ADA expressly provides that a public accommodation may exclude an individual, if that individual poses a direct threat to the health or safety of others that cannot be mitigated by appropriate modifications in the public accommodation's policies or procedures, or by the provision of auxiliary aids. A public accommodation will be permitted to establish objective safety criteria for the operation of its business; however, any safety standard must be based on objective requirements rather than stereotypes or generalizations about the ability of persons with disabilities to participate in an activity.

Are there any limits on the kinds of modifications in policies, practices, and procedures required by the ADA?

Yes. The ADA does not require modifications that would fundamentally alter the nature of the services provided by the public accommodation. For example, it would not be discriminatory for a physician specialist who treats only burn patients to refer a deaf individual to another physician for treatment of a broken limb or respiratory ailment. To require a physician to accept patients outside of his or her specialty would fundamentally alter the nature of the medical practice.

What kinds of auxiliary aids and services are required by the ADA to ensure effective communication with individuals with hearing or vision impairments?

Appropriate auxiliary aids and services may include services and devices such as qualified interpreters, assistive listening devices, notetakers, and written materials for individuals with hearing impairments; and qualified readers, taped texts, and Brailled or large print materials for individuals with vision impairments.

Are there any limitations on the ADA's auxiliary aids requirements?

Yes. The ADA does not require the provision of any auxiliary aid that would result in an undue burden or in a fundamental alteration in the nature of the goods or services provided by a public accommodation. However, the public accommodation is not relieved from the duty to furnish an alternative auxiliary aid, if available, that would not result in a fundamental alteration or undue burden. Both of these limitations are derived from existing regulations and case-law under section 504 and are to be determined on a case-by-case basis.

Will restaurants be required to have Brailled menus?

No, not if waiters or other employees are made available to read the menu to a blind customer.

Will a clothing store be required to have Brailled price tags?

No. Sales personnel could provide price information orally upon request.

Will a bookstore be required to maintain a sign language interpreter on its staff in order to communicate with deaf customers?

No, not if employees communicate by pen and notepad when necessary.

Are there any limitations on the ADA's barrier removal requirements for existing facilities?

Yes. Barrier removal need only be accomplished when it is "readily achievable" to do so.

What does the term "readily achievable" mean?

It means "easily accomplishable and able to be carried out without much difficulty or expense."

What are examples of the types of modifications that would be readily achievable in most cases?

Examples include the simple ramping of a few steps, the installation of grab bars where only routine reinforcement of the wall is required, the lowering of telephones, and similar modest adjustments.

Will businesses need to rearrange furniture and display racks?

Possibly. For example, restaurants may need to rearrange tables and department stores may need to adjust their layout of racks and shelves in order to permit wheelchair access.

Will businesses need to install elevators?

Businesses are not required to retrofit their facilities to install elevators unless such installation is readily achievable, which is unlikely in most cases.

When barrier removal is not readily achievable, what kinds of alternative steps are required by the ADA?

Alternatives may include such measures as in-store assistance for removing articles from high shelves, home delivery of groceries, or coming to the door to receive or return dry cleaning.

Must alternative steps be taken without regard to cost?

No, only readily achievable alternative steps must be undertaken.

How is "readily achievable" determined in a multi-site business?

In determining whether an action to make a public accommodation accessible would be "readily achievable," the overall size of the parent corporation or entity is only one factor to be considered. The ADA also permits consideration of the financial resources of the particular facility or facilities involved and the administrative or fiscal relationship of the facility or facilities to the parent entity.

Who has responsibility for removing barriers in a shopping mall, the landlord who owns the mall or the tenant who leases the store?

Legal responsibility for removing barriers depends upon who has legal authority to make alterations, which is generally determined by the contractual agreement between the landlord and tenant. In most cases the landlord will have full control over common areas.

What does the ADA require in new construction?

The ADA requires that all new construction of places of public accommodation, as well as of "commercial facilities" such as office buildings, be accessible. Elevators are generally not required in facilities under three stories or with fewer than 3,000 square feet per floor, unless the building is a shopping center, mall, or professional office of a health care provider.

Is it expensive to make all newly constructed public accommodations and commercial facilities accessible?

The cost of incorporating accessibility features in new construction is less than one percent of construction costs. This is a small price in relation to the economic benefits to be derived from full accessibility in the future, such as increased employment and consumer spending and decreased welfare dependency.

Must every feature of a new facility be accessible?

No, only a reasonable number of elements such as parking spaces and bathrooms must be made accessible in order for a facility to be "readily accessible." Moreover, mechanical areas, such as catwalks and fan rooms, to which access is required only for purposes of maintenance and repairs, might not need to be physically accessible if the essential functions of the work performed in those areas require physical mobility.

What are the ADA requirements for altering facilities?

All alterations that could affect the usability of a facility must be made in an accessible manner to the maximum extent feasible. For example, if during renovations a doorway is being relocated, the new doorway must be wide enough to meet the new construction standard for accessibility. When alterations are made to a primary function area, such as the lobby of a bank or the dining area of a cafeteria, an accessible path of travel to the altered area must also be provided. The bathrooms, telephones, and drinking fountains serving that area must also be made accessible. These additional accessibility alterations are only required to the extent that the added accessibility costs are not disproportionate to the overall cost of the alterations. Elevators are generally not required in facilities under three stories or with fewer than 3000 square feet per floor, unless the building is a shopping center, mall, or professional office of a health care provider.

Does the ADA permit a disabled person to sue a business when that individual believes that discrimination is about to occur, or must the individual wait for the discrimination to occur?

The ADA public accommodations provisions permit an individual to allege discrimination based on a disabled person's reasonable belief that discrimination is about to occur. This provision allows a person who uses a wheelchair to challenge the planned construction of a new place of public accommodation, such as a shopping mall, that would not be accessible to wheelchair users. The resolution of such challenges prior to the construction of an inaccessible facility would enable any necessary remedial measures to be incorporated in the building at the planning stage, when such changes would be relatively inexpensive.

How does the ADA affect existing State and local building codes?

Existing codes remain in effect. The ADA allows the Attorney General to certify that a State law, local building code, or similar ordinance that establishes accessibility requirements meets or exceeds the minimum accessibility requirements for public accommodations and commercial facilities. Any State or local government may apply for certification of its code or ordinance. The Attorney General can certify a code or ordinance only after prior notice and a public hearing at which interested people, including individuals with disabilities, are provided an opportunity to testify against the certification.

What is the effect of certification of a State or local code or ordinance?

Certification can be advantageous if an entity has constructed or altered a facility according to a certified code or ordinance. If someone later brings an enforcement proceeding against the entity, the certification is considered "rebuttable evidence" that the State law or local ordinance meets or exceeds the minimum requirements of the ADA. In other words, the entity can argue that the construction or alteration met the requirements of the ADA because it was done in compliance with the State or local code that had been certified.

When are the public accommodations provisions effective?

In general, they become effective on January 26, 1992.

How will the public accommodations provisions be enforced?

Private individuals may bring lawsuits in which they can obtain court orders to stop discrimination. Individuals may also file complaints with the Attorney General, who is authorized to bring lawsuits in cases of general public importance or where a "pattern or practice" of discrimination is alleged. In these cases, the Attorney General may seek monetary damages and civil penalties. Civil penalties may not exceed $50,000 for a first violation or $100,000 for any subsequent violation.

Miscellaneous

What is the relationship between the ADA and the Rehabilitation Act of 1973?

The Rehabilitation Act of 1973 prohibits discrimination on the basis of handicap by the federal government, federal contractors and by recipients of federal financial assistance. If you were covered by the Rehabilitation Act prior to the passage of the ADA, the ADA will not affect that coverage. Many of the provisions contained in the ADA are based on Section 504 of the Rehabilitation Act and its implementing regulations. If you are receiving federal financial assistance and are in compliance with Section 504, you are probably in compliance with the ADA requirements affecting employment except in those areas where the ADA contains additional requirements. Your nondiscrimination requirements as a federal contractor under Section 503 of the Rehabilitation Act will be essentially the same as those under the ADA; however, you will continue to have additional affirmative action requirements under Section 503 that do not exist under the ADA.

Is the Federal government covered by the ADA?

The ADA does not cover the executive branch of the Federal Government. The executive branch continues to be covered by title V of the Rehabilitation Act of 1973, which prohibits discrimination in services and employment on the basis of handicap and which is a model for the requirements of the ADA. The ADA, however, does cover Congress and other entities in the legislative branch of the Federal Government.

What requirements, other than those mandating nondiscrimination in employment, does the ADA place on State and local governments?

All government facilities, services, and communications must be accessible consistent with the requirements of section 504 of the Rehabilitation Act of 1973. Individuals may file complaints with Federal agencies to be desigated by the Attorney General or bring private lawsuits.

Does the ADA cover private apartments and private homes?

The ADA generally does not cover private residential facilities. These facilities are addressed in the Fair Housing Amendments Act of 1988, which prohibits discrimination on the basis of disability in selling or renting housing. If a building contains both residential and nonresidential portions, only the nonresidential portions are covered by the ADA. For example, in a large hotel that has a residential apartment wing, the residential wing would be covered by the Fair Housing Act and the other rooms would be covered by the ADA.

Does the ADA cover air transportation?

Discrimination by air carriers is not covered by the ADA but rather by the Air Carrier Access Act.

What are the ADA's requirements for public transit buses?

The ADA requires the Department of Transportation to issue regulations mandating accessible public transit vehicles and facilities. The regulations must include a requirement that all new fixed-route, public transit buses be accessible and that supplementary paratransit services be provided for those individuals with disabilities who cannot use fixed-route bus service.

How will the ADA make telecommunications accessible?

The ADA requires the establishment of telephone relay services for individuals who use telecommunications devices for the deaf (TDD's) or similar devices. The Federal Communications Commission will issue regulations specifying standards for the operation of these services.

Are businesses entitled to any tax benefit to help pay for the cost of compliance?

As amended in 1990, the Internal Revenue Code allows a deduction of up to $15,000 per year for expenses associated with the removal of qualified architectural and transportation barriers.

The 1990 amendment also permits eligible small businesses to receive a tax credit for certain costs of compliance with the ADA. An eligible small business is one whose gross receipts do not exceed $1,000,000 or whose workforce does not consist of more than 30 full-time workers. Qualifying businesses may claim a credit of up to 50 percent of eligible access expenditures that exceed $250 but do not exceed $10,250. Examples of eligible access expenditures include the necessary and reasonable costs of removing architectural, physical, communications, and transportation barriers; providing readers, interpreters, and other auxiliary aids; and acquiring or modifying equipment or devices.

LEGISLATIVE PROCESS

This section on the Legislative Process is drawn from
U.S. Senate Report 101-116, dated August 30, 1989

Legislative Process

On August 2, 1989, the Senate Committee on Labor and Human Resources, by a vote of 16-0, ordered favorably reported S. 933, the Americans with Disabilities Act of 1989 (the ADA).

The bill's chief sponsor is Senator Tom Harkin, chairman of the Subcommittee on the Handicapped.

Hearings

Hearings were held before the Senate Labor and Human Resources Committee and the Labor and Human Resources' Subcommittee on the Handicapped on legislation to establish a clear and comprehensive prohibition of discrimination on the basis of disability between September 27, 1988 and June 22, 1989.

On September 27, 1988, a joint hearing was held before the Subcommittee on the Handicapped and the House of Representatives' Subcommittee on Select Education on S. 2345, the Americans with Disabilities Act of 1988. Testifying witnesses represented the National Council on the Handicapped; the President's Commission on the Human Immunodeficiency Virus Epidemic; the World Institute on Disability; Gallaudet University; and the Organization for Use of the Telephone. Others testifying included Mary Linden of Morton Grove, Illinois who lived in an institution; Dan Piper, an 18-year old with Down's Syndrome and Sylvia Piper of Ankeny, Iowa; Jade Calegory, a 12-year old movie actor with Spina Bifida from Corona Del Mar, California; Lakisha Griffin from Talladega, Alabama, who attends the Alabama School for the Blind; Belinda Mason from Tobinsport, Indiana who has AIDS; and W. Mitchell from Denver, Colorado, who uses a wheelchair and who was severely burned.

On May 9, 1989, the Committee on Labor and Human Resources held a hearing on S. 933, the Americans with Disabilities Act of 1989. Testifying witnesses represented Gallaudet University; the Task Force on the Rights and Empowerment of Americans with Disabilities; the President's Committee on Employment of People with Disabilities; the U.S. Chamber of Commerce; the American Society of Personnel Administrators; the Disability Rights Education and Defense Fund; the National Coalition for Cancer Survivorship; the Department of Legislation, AFL-CIO; the Associated General Contractors of America; and the National Organizations Responding to AIDS.

Others testifying included Tony Coelho, the Majority Whip of the House of Representatives; Mary DeSapio, a cancer survivor; Joseph Danowsky, an attorney who is blind; and Amy Dimsdale, a college graduate who is quadriplegic and who after 5 years of looking for work remains unemployed.

On May 10, the Subcommittee on the Handicapped heard testimony from witnesses representing the Paralyzed Veterans of America; Advocating Change Together; Barrier Free Environments; the Association of Christian Schools International; the National Federation of Independent Business; the National Association of Theater Owners; the National Easter Seal Society; the National Technical Institute for the Deaf; the Minnesota Relay Service; AT&T; the American Civil Liberties Union; the State of New York Public Service Commission; and the National Association of Regulatory Utility Commissioners. Others testifying included Bob Dole, Senator from Kansas and Senate Minority Leader; Lisa Carl who has cerebral palsy and her mother, Vickie Franke; the Honorable Neil Hartigan, Attorney General of the State of Illinois; Betty and Emory

Corey, Baltimore, Maryland; and Ilene Foster, Baltimore, Maryland.

On May 16, the Subcommittee on the Handicapped heard testimony from representatives of the Queens Independent Living Center; ADAPT; the Columbia Lighthouse for the Blind; Disability Services; the Virginia Association of Public Transit Officials; the Cambria County Transit Authority; the American Public Transit Association; the American Bus Association; the Eastern Paralyzed Veterans of America; the National Disability Action Center; the Virginia Council for Independent Living; the United Bus Owners of America; and Greyhound Lines, Inc.

On June 22, the Labor and Human Resources Committee heard testimony from Richard L. Thornburgh, Attorney General of the United States, and Senator Lowell P. Weicker, Jr., chief sponsor of the Americans with Disabilities Act of 1988.

Need for the Legislation

The Committee, after extensive review and analysis over a number of Congresses, concludes that there exists a compelling need to establish a clear and comprehensive Federal prohibition of discrimination on the basis of disability in the areas of employment in the private sector, public accommodations, public services, transportation, and telecommunications.

Summary of Committee Action

S. 933 was brought for markup at the Committee on Labor and Human Resources executive session on August 2, 1989.

The Committee voted to adopt and report S. 933, as amended, by a roll call vote of 16-0.

Explanation of the Legislation

Definition of the Term "Disability"

The definition of the term "disability" included in the bill is comparable to the definition of the term "individual with handicaps" in section 7(8)(B) of the Rehabilitation Act of 1973 and section 802(h) of the Fair Housing Act.

It is the Committee's intent that the analysis of the term "individual with handicaps" by the Department of Health, Education, and Welfare of the regulations implementing section 504 and the analysis by the Department of Housing and Urban Development of the regulations implementing the Fair Housing Amendments Act of 1988 apply to the definition of the term "disability" included in this legislation.

The use of the term "disability" instead of "handicap" and the term "individual with a disability" instead of "individual with handicaps" represents an effort by the Committee to make use of up-to-date, currently accepted terminology. In regard to this legislation, as well as in other contexts, the Congress has been apprised of the fact that to many individuals with disabilities the terminology applied to them is a very significant and sensitive issue.

As with racial and ethnic epithets, the choice of terms to apply to a person with a disability is overlaid with stereotypes, patronizing attitudes, and other emotional connotations. Many individuals with disabilities and organizations representing them object to the use of such terms as "handicapped person" or "the handicapped." In recent legislation, Congress has begun to recognize this shift of terminology, e.g., by changing the name of the National Council on the Handicapped to the National Council on Disability.

The Committee concluded that it was important for the current legislation to use terminology most in line with the sensibilities of most Americans with disabilities. No change in definition or substance is intended nor should be attributed to this change in phraseology.

THE ADA

The Summary and Analysis in this section are drawn from

U.S. Senate Report 101-116, dated August 30, 1989

and

U.S. House of Representatives Report 101-485, Parts I-IV, dated May 14-15, 1990

*The text of the Americans with Disabilities Act
in this section is drawn from
Volume 104 of United States Statutes at Large*

SUMMARY

The purpose of the ADA is to provide a clear and comprehensive national mandate to end discrimination against individuals with disabilities and to bring persons with disabilities into the economic and social mainstream of American life; to provide enforceable standards addressing discrimination against individuals with disabilities, and to ensure that the Federal government plays a central role in enforcing these standards on behalf of individuals with disabilities.

The ADA defines "disability" to mean, with respect to an individual: a physical or mental impairment that substantially limits one or more of the major life activities of such individual, a record of such an impairment, or being regarded as having such an impairment.

Title I

Title I of the ADA specifies that an employer, employment agency, labor organization, or joint labor-management committee may not discriminate against any qualified individual with a disability in regard to any term, condition or privilege of employment. The ADA incorporates many of the standards of discrimination set out in regulations implementing section 504 of the Rehabilitation Act of 1973, including the obligation to provide reasonable accommodations unless it would result in an undue hardship on the operation of the business.

The ADA incorporates by reference the enforcement provisions under Title VII of the Civil Rights Act of 1964 (including injunctive relief and back pay). Title I goes into effect two years after the date of enactment. For the first two years after the effective date, employers with 25 or more employees are covered. Thereafter, employers with 15 or more employees are covered.

Title II

Title II of the ADA specifies that no qualified individual with a disability may be discriminated against by a department, agency, special purpose district, or other instrumentality of a State or a local government. In addition to a general prohibition against discrimination, title II includes specific requirements applicable to public transportation provided by public transit authorities. Finally, title II incorporates by reference the enforcement provisions in section 505 of the Rehabilitation Act of 1973.

With respect to public transportation, all new fixed route buses must be made accessible unless a transit authority can demonstrate that no lifts are available from qualified manufacturers. A public transit authority must also provide paratransit for those individuals who cannot use mainline accessible transportation up to the point where the provision of such supplementary services would pose an undue financial burden on a transit authority.

Title II takes effect 18 months after the date of enactment, with the exception of Sections 242 and 244, which become effective on the date of enactment of the ADA.

Title III

Title III of the ADA specifies that no individual shall be discriminated against in the full and equal enjoyment of the goods, services, facilities, privileges, advantages, and accommodations of any place of public accommodation operated by a private entity on the basis of a disability.

Public accommodations include: restaurants, hotels, doctor's offices, pharmacies, grocery stores, shopping centers, and other similar establishments.

Existing facilities must be made accessible if the changes are "readily achievable," i.e., easily accomplishable without much difficulty or expense. Auxiliary aids and services must be provided unless such provision would fundamentally alter the nature of the program or cause an undue burden. New construction and major renovations must be designed and constructed to be readily accessible to and usable by people with disabilities. Elevators need not be installed if the building has less than three stories or has less than 3,000 square feet per floor except if the building is a shopping center, shopping mall, or offices for health care providers or if the Attorney General decides that other categories of buildings require the installation of elevators.

Title III also includes specific prohibitions on discrimination in public transportation services provided by private entities.

The provisions of title III become effective 18 months after the date of enactment. Title III incorporates enforcement provisions in private actions comparable to the applicable enforcement provisions in title II of the Civil Rights Act of 1964 (injunctive relief) and provides for pattern and practice cases by the Attorney General, including authority to seek monetary damages and civil penalties.

Title IV

Title IV of the ADA specifies that telephone services offered to the general public must include interstate and intrastate telecommunication relay services so that such services provide individuals who use nonvoice terminal devices because of disabilities (such as deaf persons) with opportunities for communications that are equivalent to those provided to individuals able to use voice telephone services.

Title V

Title V of the ADA includes miscellaneous provisions, including a construction clause explaining the relationship between the provisions in the ADA and the provisions in other Federal and State laws; a construction clause explaining that the ADA does not disrupt the current nature of insurance underwriting; a prohibition against retaliation; a clear statement that States are not immune from actions in Federal court for a violation of the ADA; a directive to the Architectural and Transportation Barriers Compliance Board to issue guidelines; and authority to award attorney's fees.

Definitions

As used in this Act:

(1) Auxiliary Aids and Services. The term "auxiliary aids and services" includes

(A) qualified interpreters or other effective methods of making aurally delivered materials available to individuals with hearing impairments;

(B) qualified readers, taped texts, or other effective methods of making visually delivered materials available to individuals with visual impairments;

(C) acquisition or modification of equipment or devices; and

(D) other similar services and actions.

(2) Disability. The term "disability" means, with respect to an individual

(A) a physical or mental impairment that substantially limits one or more of the major life activities of such individual;

(B) a record of such an impairment; or

(C) being regarded as having such an impairment.

If an individual meets any one of these three tests, he or she is considered to be an individual with a disability for purposes of coverage under the ADA.

Test A. *Under the first test, an individual must have a physical or mental impairment. This means any physiological disorder or condition, cosmetic disfigurement, or anatomical loss affecting one or more of the following body systems: neurological; musculoskeletal; special sense organs; respiratory, including speech organs; cardiovascular; reproductive, digestive; genito-urinary; hemic and lymphatic; skin; and endocrine. It also means any mental or psychological disorder, such as mental retardation, organic brain syndrome, emotional or mental illness, and specific learning disabilities.*

Although the definition does not include a list of all the specific conditions, diseases, or infections that would constitute physical or mental impairments, examples include: orthopedic, visual, speech and hearing impairments; cerebral palsy; epilepsy; infection with the Human Immunodeficiency Virus; muscular dystrophy; multiple sclerosis; cancer; heart disease; diabetes; mental retardation; emotional illness; specific learning disabilities; drug addiction and alcoholism.

Physical or mental impairment does not include simple physical characteristics, such as blue eyes or black hair. Nor does it include environmental, cultural or economic disadvantages, such as having a prison record, or being poor. Age is not a disability. However, a person who has these characteristics and also has a physical or mental impairment may be considered as having a disability for purposes of the ADA based on the impairment.

Under the first test, the impairment must be one that "substantially limits a major life activity." Major life activities include such things as caring for one's self, performing manual tasks, walking, seeing, hearing, speaking, breathing, learning and working.

For example, a paraplegic is substantially limited in the major life activity of walking, a person who is blind is substantially limited in the major life activity of seeing, and a person who is mentally retarded is substantially limited in the major life activity of learning.

The impairment should be assessed without considering whether mitigating measures, such as auxiliary aids or reasonable accommodations, would result in a less-than-substantial limitation. For example, a person with epilep-

sy, an impairment which substantially limits a major life activity, is covered under this test, even if the effects of the impairment which substantially limits a major life activity, is also covered, even if the hearing loss is corrected by the use of a hearing aid.

A person with an impairment who is discriminated against in employment is also limited in the major life activity of working. However, a person who is limited in his or her ability to perform only a particular job, because of circumstances unique to that job site or the materials used, may not be substantially limited in the major life activity of working. For example, an applicant whose trade is painting would not be substantially limited in the major life activity of working if he has a mild allergy to a specialized paint used by one employer which is not generally used in the field in which the painter works.

However, if a person is employed as a painter and is assigned to work with a unique paint which caused severe allergies, such as skin rashes or seizures, the person would be substantially limited in a major life activity, by virtue of the resulting skin disease or seizure disorder. The cause of a disability is always irrelevant to the determination of disability. In such a case, a reasonable accommodation to the employee may include assignment to other areas where the particular paint is not used.

Test B. This test is intended to cover those who have a record of an impairment. This includes a person who has a history of an impairment that substantially limited a major life activity, such as those who have recovered from an impairment. It also includes persons who have been misclassified as having an impairment. Examples include *a person who had, but no longer has, cancer, or a person who was misclassified as being mentally retarded.*

Test C. *This test is intended to cover persons who are treated by a covered entity as having a physical or mental impairment that substantially limits a major life activity. It applies whether or not a person has an impairment, if that person was treated as if he or she had an impairment that substantially limits a major life activity.*

The ADA uses the same "regarded as" test set forth in the regulations implementing Section 504 of the Rehabilitation Act.

The perception of the covered entity is a key element of this test. A person who perceives himself to have an impairment, but does not have an impairment, and is not treated as if he has an impairment, is not protected under this test.

A person would be covered under this test if an employer refused to hire, or a restaurant refused to serve, that person because of a fear of "negative reactions" of others to that person. A person would also be covered if an entity perceived that the applicant had an impairment which prevented the person from working, or if a public accommodation refused to serve a patron because it perceived that the patron had an impairment that limited his or her enjoyment of the goods or services being offered.

For example, severe burn victims often face discrimination in employment and participation in community activities which results in substantial limitation of major life activities. These persons would be covered under this test because of the attitudes of others towards the impairment, even if they did not view themselves as "impaired."

The rationale for this third test, as used in the Rehabilitation Act of 1973, was articulated by the Supreme Court in School Board of Nassau County v. Arline. *The Court noted that although an individual may have an impairment that does not in fact substantially limit a major life activity, the reaction of others may prove just as disabling. "Such an impairment might not diminish a person's physical or mental capabilities, but could nevertheless substantially limit that person's ability to work as a result of the negative reactions of others to the impairment."*

The Court concluded that, by including this test, "Congress acknowledged that society's accumulated myths and fears about disability and diseases are as handicapping as are the physical limitations that flow from actual impairment."

Thus, a person who is rejected from a job because of the myths, fears and stereotypes associated with disabilities would be covered under this third test, whether or not the employer's perception was shared by others in the field and whether or not the person's physical or mental condition would be considered a disability under the first or second part of the definition.

Behaviors and conditions not included as disabilities

Current illegal use of drugs is not protected under the bill. Homosexuality and bisexuality, which were never covered disabilities under other federal disability laws, because they are not physical or mental impairments, are ex-

plicitly noted as not being impairments and as such are not disabilities under the ADA. Transvestism, transsexualism, pedophilia, exhibitionism, voyeurism, gender identity disorders not resulting from physical impairments, other sexual behavior disorders, compulsive gambling, kleptomania, pyromania, and psychoactive substance use disorders resulting from current illegal use of drugs, are also excluded.

(3) State. The term "State" means each of the several States, the District of Columbia, the Commonwealth of Puerto Rico, Guam, American Samoa, the Virgin Islands, the Trust Territory of the Pacific Islands, and the Commonwealth of the Northern Mariana Islands.

TEXT AND ANALYSIS OF THE AMERICANS WITH DISABILITIES ACT

The text of the law appears in normal type; the analysis appears in italic type.

Section 1. Short Title

This Act may be cited as the "Americans with Disabilities Act of 1990."

The use of the term "disabilities" instead of the term "handicaps" reflects the desire of the House Committee on the Judiciary to use the most current terminology. It reflects the preference of persons with disabilities to use that term rather than "handicapped" as used in previous laws, such as the Rehabilitation Act of 1973 and the Fair Housing Amendments Act of 1988.

By this change in phraseology, the Committee does not intend to change the substantive definition of handicap.

The ADA should also not be interpreted to be limited to "Americans" with disabilities. The use of the title "Americans with Disabilities" reflects the belief that individuals with disabilities compose an integral part of our nation's makeup, and, like all other individuals, are entitled to equal access and opportunity. As in other civil rights laws, however, the ADA should not be interpreted to mean that only American citizens are entitled to the protections afforded by the Act.

Title I - Employment

TITLE I. EMPLOYMENT

Section 101. Definitions

As used in this title:

(1) Commission. The term "Commission" means the Equal Employment Opportunity Commission established by section 705 of the Civil Rights Act of 1964.

(2) Covered Entity. The term "covered entity" means an employer, employment agency, labor organization, or joint labor-management committee.

(3) Direct Threat. The term "direct threat" means a significant risk to the health or safety of others that cannot be eliminated by reasonable accommodation.

(4) Employee. The term "employee" means an individual employed by an employer.

(5) Employer.

(A) In General. The term "employer" means a person engaged in an industry affecting commerce who has 15 or more employees for each working day in each of 20 or more calendar weeks in the current or preceding calendar year, and any agent of such person, except that, for two years following the effective date of this title, an employer means a person engaged in an industry affecting commerce who has 25 or more employees for each working day in each of 20 or more calendar weeks in the current or preceding year, and any agent of such person.

(B) Exceptions. The term "employer" does not include

(i) the United States, a corporation wholly owned by the government of the United States, or an Indian tribe; or

(ii) a bona fide private membership club (other than a labor organization) that is exempt from taxation under section 501(c) of the Internal Revenue Code of 1986.

(6) Illegal Use of Drugs.

(A) In General. The term "illegal use of drugs" means the use of drugs, the possession or distribution of which is unlawful under the Controlled Substances Act. Such term does not include the use of a drug taken under supervision by a licensed health care professional, or other uses authorized by the Controlled Substances Act or other provisions of Federal law.

(B) Drugs. The term "drug" means a controlled substance, as defined in schedules I through V of section 202 of the Controlled Substances Act.

(7) Person, Etc. The terms "person", "labor organization", "employment agency", "commerce", and "industry affecting commerce", shall have the same meaning given such terms in section 701 of the Civil Rights Act of 1964.

(8) Qualified Individual with a Disability. The term "qualified individual with a disability" means an individual with a disability who, with or without reasonable accommodation, can perform the essential functions of the employment position that such individual holds or desires.

For the purposes of this title, consideration shall be given to the employer's judgment as to what functions of a job are essential, and if an employer has prepared a written description before advertising or interviewing applicants for the job, this description shall be considered evidence of the essential functions of the job.

(9) Reasonable Accommodation. The term "reasonable accommodation" may include

(A) making existing facilities used by employees readily accessible to and usable by individuals with disabilities; and

(B) job restructuring, part-time or modified work schedules, reassignment to a vacant position, acquisition or modification of equipment or devices, appropriate adjustment or modifications of examinations, training materials or policies, the provision of qualified readers or interpreters, and other similar accommodations for individuals with disabilities.

(10) Undue Hardship.

(A) In General. The term "undue hardship" means an action requiring significant difficulty or expense, when considered in light of the factors set forth in subparagraph (B).

(B) Factors to be Considered. In determining whether an accommodation would impose an undue hardship on a covered entity, factors to be considered include

(i) the nature and cost of the accommodation needed under this Act;

(ii) the overall financial resources of the facility or facilities involved in the provision of the reasonable accommodation; the number of persons employed at such facility; the effect on expenses and resources, or the impact otherwise of such accommodation upon the operation of the facility;

(iii) the overall financial resources of the covered entity; the overall size of the business of a covered entity with respect to the number of its employees; the number, type, and location of its facilities; and

(iv) the type of operation or operations of the covered entity, including the composition, structure, and functions of the workforce of such entity; the geographic separateness, administrative, or fiscal relationship of the facility or facilities in question to the covered entity.

Title I prohibits discrimination in employment against a qualified person with a disability. The title borrows much of its procedural framework from title VII of the Civil Rights Act of 1964, which prohibits discrimination in employment on the basis of race, color, religion, sex or national origin, by incorporating title VII's enforcement provisions, notice posting provisions, and employer coverage provisions. The title borrows much of its substantive framework from Section 504 of the Rehabilitation Act of 1973.

The underlying premise of this title is that persons with disabilities should not be excluded from job opportunities unless they are actually unable to do the job. The requirement that job criteria actually measure skills required by the job is a critical protection, because stereotypes and misconceptions about the abilities and inabilities of persons with disabilities continue to be pervasive. Discrimination occurs against persons with disabilities because of stereotypes, discomfort, misconceptions, and fears about increased costs and decreased productivity.

In order to assure a match between job criteria and an applicant's actual ability to do the job, the bill contains the following provisions:

the requirement that persons with disabilities not be disqualified because of the inability to perform nonessential or marginal functions of the job;

the requirement that any selection criteria that screen out or tend to screen out people with disabilities be job-related and consistent with business necessity; and

the requirement to provide reasonable accommodation to assist persons with disabilities to meet legitimate job criteria.

These requirements work together to eliminate the pervasive bias against employing persons with disabilities.

If a person with a disability applies for a job and meets all selection criteria except one that he or she cannot meet because of a disability, the criterion must concern an essential, and not marginal, aspect of the job. The criterion must be carefully tailored to measure the actual ability of a person to perform an essential function of the job. If the criterion meets this test, it is not discriminatory on its face and is not prohibited by the ADA. If the legitimate criterion can be satisfied by the applicant with a reasona-

ble accommodation, then the reasonable accommodation
must be provided.

The term "qualified individual with a disability" means an
individual with a disability who, with a reasonable accommodation if necessary, can perform the essential functions
of the employment position that such individual holds or
desires.

"[I]nclusion of this phrase is useful in emphasizing that
handicapped persons should not be disqualified simply because they may have difficulty in performing tasks that
bear only a marginal relationship to a particular job."

For example, many employers require driver's licenses for
a variety of jobs which do not require driving or where
driving is incidental to the job. A driver's license is often
required because it is presumed that people who drive to
work are more likely to arrive at work on time or because
a driver can do an occasional errand. The "essential functions" requirement assures that a person who cannot drive
because of his or her disability is not disqualified for
these reasons if he or she can do the actual duties of the
job.

In one case, a person with epilepsy applied for the job of
group counselor at a juvenile hall. After receiving a job
offer, the offer was withdrawn when the employer
learned that the applicant did not have a driver's license.
Driving was required for emergencies, to take a juvenile
to the hospital, for example, and to transport the juveniles
to court appearances. While it was necessary that some of
the group counselors be able to drive, it was not essential
that all group counselors be available to drive. On any
given shift, another group counselor could perform the

driving duty. Hence, it is necessary to review the job duty not in isolation, but in the context of the actual work environment.

The incorporation of the requirement of reasonable accommodation into the definition of "qualified individual with a disability" is meant to indicate that essential functions are those which must be performed, even if the manner in which particular job tasks comprising those functions are performed, or the equipment used in performing them, may be different for an employee with a disability than for a non-disabled employee. For example, in a job requiring the use of a computer, the essential function is the ability to access, input, and retrieve information from the computer. It is not "essential" that a person be able to use the keyboard or visually read the information from a computer screen. Adaptive equipment or software may enable a person with no arms or a person with impaired vision to control the computer and access information.

The determination of whether a person is qualified should be made at the time of the employment action, e.g., hiring or promotion, and should not be based on the possibility that the employee or applicant will become incapacitated and unqualified in the future. Nor can paternalistic concerns about what is best for the person with a disability serve to foreclose employment opportunities.

[A] person with a disability applying for or currently holding a job subject to these standards must be able to satisfy any physical qualification standard that is job-related and required by business necessity in order to be considered a qualified individual with a disability.

Section 102. Discrimination

(a) General Rule. No covered entity shall discriminate against a qualified individual with a disability because of the disability of such individual in regard to job application procedures, the hiring, advancement, or discharge of employees, employee compensation, job training, and other terms, conditions, and privileges of employment.

As with other civil rights laws prohibiting discrimination in employment, the House Committee on the Judiciary does not intend to limit the ability of covered entities to choose and maintain a qualified workforce. Covered entities continue to have the ability to hire and employ employees who can perform the job. Employers can continue to use job-related criteria in choosing qualified employees. For example, in a job that requires lifting 50 pound boxes, an employer may test applicants and employees to determine whether they can lift 50 pound boxes. Similarly, an employer can continue to give typists typing tests to determine their abilities.

The Committee does not intend that covered entities have an obligation to prefer applicants with disabilities over other applicants on the basis of disability.

(b) Construction. As used in subsection (a), the term "discriminate" includes

(1) limiting, segregating, or classifying a job applicant or employee in a way that adversely affects the opportunities or status of such applicant or employee because of the disability of such applicant or employee;

[A]n employer could not adopt a different pay scale, benefits, promotion opportunities or working area for employees with disabilities. In one case, an employer had a separate job category for janitors with developmental disabilities with lower pay, no benefits or seniority rights, even though the job duties were the same as other janitors. This would be a violation of this title.

(2) participating in a contractual or other arrangement or relationship that has the effect of subjecting a covered entity's qualified applicant or employee with a disability to the discrimination prohibited by this title (such relationship includes a relationship with an employment or referral agency, labor union, an organization providing fringe benefits to an employee of the covered entity, or an organization providing training and apprenticeship programs);

[A]ssume that an employer contracts with a hotel for a conference held for the employer's employees. Under the Act, the employer has an affirmative duty to investigate the accessibility of a location that it plans to use for its own employees. Suggested approaches for determining accessibility would be for the employer to inspect the hotel first-hand, if possible, or to ask a local disability group to inspect the hotel. In any event, the employer can always protect itself in such situations by simply ensuring that the contract with the hotel specifies that all rooms to be used for the conference, including the exhibit and meeting rooms, be accessible in accordance with applicable standards. If the hotel breaches this accessibility provision, the hotel will be liable to the employer for the cost of any accommodation needed to provide access to the disabled individual

during the conference, as well as for any other costs accrued by the employer. Placing a duty on the employer to investigate the accessibility of places that it contracts for will, in all likelihood, by the impetus for ensuring that these types of contractual provisions become commonplace in our society.

(3) utilizing standards, criteria, or methods of administration

(A) that have the effect of discrimination on the basis of disability; or

(B) that perpetuate the discrimination of others who are subject to common administrative control;

[E]mployers may not deny health insurance coverage completely to an individual based on the person's diagnosis or disability. For example, it is permissible for an employer to offer insurance policies that limit coverage for certain procedures or treatments (e.g., a limit on the extent of kidneys dialysis or whether dialysis will be covered at all, or a limit on the amount of blood transfusions or whether transfusions will be covered). It would not be permissible, however, to deny coverage to individuals, such as persons with kidney disease or hemophilia, who are affected by these limits on coverage for procedures or treatments, for other procedures or treatments connected with their disability. It would also not be permissible to deny coverage to such individuals for other conditions not connected with these limitations on coverage, such as treatment for a broken leg or heart surgery. While limitation may be placed on reimbursements for a procedure or the types of drugs or procedures covered, that limitation must apply

to all persons, with or without disabilities. Persons with disabilities must have equal access to the health insurance coverage that is provided by the employer to all employees.

For example, an employer could not enter into a contract for liability insurance with an insurance company who refused to cover accidents or injuries of persons with disabilities. Nor could the employer refuse to hire a person with a disability because the liability policy did not cover persons with disabilities.

(4) excluding or otherwise denying equal jobs or benefits to a qualified individual because of the known disability of an individual with whom the qualified individual is known to have a relationship or association;

This provision protects persons who associate with persons with disabilities and who are discriminated against because of that association.

This provision applies only when the employer knows of the association with the other person and knows of that other person's disability. The burden of proof is on the individual claiming discrimination to prove that the discrimination was motivated by that individual's relationship or association with a person with a disability.

For example, it would be discriminatory for an employer to discriminate against a qualified employee who did volunteer work for people with AIDS, if the employer knew of the employee's relationship or association with the people with AIDS, and if the employment action was motivated by that relationship or association.

Similarly, it would be illegal for an employer to discriminate against a qualified employee because that employee had a family member or a friend who had a disability, if the employer knew about the relationship or association, knew that the friend or family member has a disability, and acted on that basis. Thus, if an employee had a spouse with a disability, and the employer took an adverse action against the employee based on the spouse's disability, this would then constitute discrimination.

This section would not apply if the employer did not know of the relationship or association, or if the employer did not know of the disability of the other person. Thus, if an employer fired an employee, and did not know of a relationship or association of the employee with a person with a disability, the employee could not claim discrimination under this section.

(5)(A) not making reasonable accommodations to the known physical or mental limitations of an otherwise qualified individual with a disability who is an applicant or employee, unless such covered entity can demonstrate that the accommodation would impose an undue hardship on the operation of the business of such covered entity; or

(B) denying employment opportunities to a job applicant or employee who is an otherwise qualified individual with a disability, if such denial is based on the need of such covered entity to make reasonable accommodation to the physical or mental impairments of the employee or applicant;

The employee or applicant must request a reasonable accommodation; the employer is not liable for failing to provide an accommodation if it was not requested.

A reasonable accommodation should be tailored to the needs of the individual and the requirements of the job. Persons with disabilities have vast experience in all aspects of their lives with the types of accommodations which are effective for them. Employers should not assume that accommodations are required without consulting the applicant or employee with the disability. Stereotypes about disability can result in stereotypes about the need for accommodations, which may exceed what is actually required. Consultations between employers and the persons with disabilities will result in an accurate assessment of what is required in order to perform the job duties.

In the event there are two effective accommodations, the employer may choose the accommodation that is less expensive or easier for the employer to implement, as long as the selected accommodation provides meaningful equal employment opportunity for the applicant or employee.

[T]he ADA provides that the employer is not required to provide accommodations if the employer demonstrates that providing such an accommodation will pose an undue hardship on the operation of its business.

The ADA defines "undue hardship" to mean an action requiring significant difficulty or expense. [A] definition of undue hardship was included in order to distinguish it from the definition of "readily achievable" in title III governing the requirement to alter existing public accommodations. Readily achievable means "easily accomplishable and able to be carried out without much difficulty or expense." The duty to provide reasonable accommodations, by contrast, is a much higher standard than the duty to remove barriers in existing buildings (if removing the barriers is readily achievable) and creates a more substantial obligation on the employer.

The determination of undue hardship is a factual one which must be made on a case-by-case basis. Like Section 504 of the Rehabilitation Act, the burden is on the employer to demonstrate that the needed accommodation would cause an undue hardship.

(6) using qualification standards, employment tests or other selection criteria that screen out or tend to screen out an individual with a disability or a class of individuals with disabilities unless the standard, test or other selection criteria, as used by the covered entity, is shown to be job-related for the position in question and is consistent with business necessity; and

If an employer uses a facially neutral qualification standard, employment test or other selection criterion that has a discriminatory effect on persons with disabilities, this practice would be discriminatory unless the employer can demonstrate that it is job-related and required by business necessity.

The requirement that job selection procedures be job-related and consistent with business necessity underscores the need to examine all selection criteria to assure that they not only provide an accurate measure of an applicant's actual ability to perform the job, but

that even if they do provide such a measure, a disabled applicant is offered a reasonable accommodation to meet the criteria that relate to the essential functions of the job at issue. It is critical that paternalistic concerns for the disabled person's own safety not be used to disqualify an otherwise qualified applicant.

(7) failing to select and administer tests concerning employment in the most effective manner to ensure that, when such test is administered to a job applicant or employee who has a disability that impairs sensory, manual, or speaking skills, such test results accurately reflect the skills, aptitude, or whatever other factor of such applicant or employee that such test purports to measure, rather than reflecting the impaired sensory, manual, or speaking skills of such employee or applicant (except where such skills are the factors that the test purports to measure).

(c) Medical Examinations and inquiries.

(1) In General. The prohibition against discrimination as referred to in subsection (a) shall include medical examinations and inquiries.

(2) Preemployment.

(A) Prohibited Examination or Inquiry. Except as provided in paragraph (3), a covered entity shall not conduct a medical examination or make inquiries of a job applicant as to whether such applicant is an individual with a disability or as to the nature or severity of such disability.

(B) Acceptable Inquiry. A covered entity may make preemployment inquiries into the ability of an applicant to perform job-related functions.

(3) Employment Entrance Examination. A covered entity may require a medical examination after an offer of employment has been made to a job applicant and prior to the commencement of the employment duties of such applicant, and may condition an offer of employment on the results of such examination, if

(A) all entering employees are subjected to such an examination regardless of disability;

(B) information obtained regarding the medical condition or history of the applicant is collected and maintained on separate forms and in separate medical files and is treated as a confidential medical record, except that

(i) supervisors and managers may be informed regarding necessary restrictions on the work or duties of the employee and necessary accommodations;

(ii) first aid and safety personnel may be informed, when appropriate, if the disability might require emergency treatment; and

(iii) government officials investigating compliance with this Act shall be provided relevant information on request; and

(C) the results of such examination are used only in accordance with this title.

(4) Examination and Inquiry.

(A) Prohibited Examinations and Inquiries. A covered entity shall not require a medical examination and shall not make inquiries of an employee as to whether such employee is an individual with a disability or as to the nature or severity of the disability, unless such examination or inquiry is shown to be job-related and consistent with business necessity.

(B) Acceptable Examinations and Inquiries. A covered entity may conduct voluntary medical examinations, including voluntary medical histories, which are part of an employee health program available to employees at that work site. A covered entity may make inquiries into the ability of an employee to perform job-related functions.

(C) Requirement. Information obtained under subparagraph (B) regarding the medical condition or history of any employee are subject to the requirements of subparagraphs (B) and (C) of paragraph (3).

Historically, employment application forms and employment interviews requested information concerning an applicant's physical or mental condition. This information was often used to exclude applicants with disabilities, particularly those with "hidden" disabilities such as epilepsy, diabetes, emotional illness, heart disease and cancer, before their ability to perform the job was even evaluated.

In order to assure that misconceptions do not bias the employment selection process, this section sets up a

*process that begins with the prohibition of preemploy-
ment medical examinations or inquiries.*

Section 103. Defenses.

(a) In General. It may be a defense to a charge of discrimination under this Act that an alleged application of qualification standards, tests, or selection criteria that screen
out or tend to screen out or otherwise deny a job or benefit to an individual with a disability has been shown to be
job-related and consistent with business necessity, and
such performance cannot be accomplished by reasonable
accommodation, as required under this title.

(b) Qualifications Standards. The term "qualification
standards" may include a requirement that an individual
shall not pose a direct threat to the health or safety of
other individuals in the workplace.

*Employers may set qualification standards for their em-
ployees. For example, an employer may have a requirement that a person be able to lift 50 pounds or be able to
drive a vehicle, if these requirements are job-related and
consistent with business necessity.*

*A qualification standard may also include a requirement
that an individual not pose a direct threat to the health or
safety of other individuals in the workplace. During consideration by the House Committee on the Judiciary, this
"direct threat" standard was extended to all individuals
with disabilities, and not simply to those with contagious
diseases or infections.*

*This concept is also contained in the Civil Rights Restora-
tion Act of 1988 and the Fair Housing Amendments Act.*

It is based on the same standard for "qualified" person with a disability that has existed for years under the Rehabilitation Act of 1973.

In order to determine whether an individual poses a direct threat to the health or safety of other individuals in the workplace, the Committee intends to use the same standard as articulated by the Supreme Court in School Board of Nassau County v. Arline. *In Arline, the court held that a "person who poses a significant risk of communicating an infectious disease to others in the workplace will not be otherwise qualified for his or her job if reasonable accommodation will not eliminate that risk." Such risk of transmitting the infection to others must be determined based on objective and accepted public health guidelines.*

Direct threat is defined as a "significant risk to the health or safety of others that cannot be eliminated with reasonable accommodation."

[A]n employer may not assume that a person with a mental disability, or a person who has been treated for a mental disability, poses a direct threat to others. This would be an assumption based on fear and stereotype. The purpose of creating the "direct threat" standard is to eliminate exclusions which are not based on objective evidence about the individual involved. Thus, in the case of a person with mental illness there must be objective evidence from the person's behavior that the person has a recent history of committing overt acts or making threats which caused harm or which directly threatened harm.

The "direct threat" standard may not be used to circumvent the prohibition against pre-employment inquiries into a person's disability. It may not be used to justify

*generalized requests or inquiries related to medical re-
cords. The prohibition against pre-offer medical examinations also applies to psychological examinations.*

*The employer may, however, conduct a post-offer medical
examination, including a psychological examination, as
long as it meets the requirements of Section 102(c)(3). If
the applicant is otherwise qualified for the job, he or she
cannot be disqualified on the basis of a physical or mental
condition unless the employer can demonstrate that the
applicant's disability poses a direct threat to others in the
workplace.*

*The determination of significant risk for persons with
disabilities must be based on the current condition of the
applicant or employee. The decision to exclude cannot be
based on merely "an elevated risk of injury."*

(c) Religious Entities.

(1) In General. This title shall not prohibit a religious
corporation, association, educational institution, or society from giving preference in employment to individuals of a particular religion to perform work connected
with the carrying on by such corporation, association,
educational institution, or society of its activities.

(2) Religious Tenets Requirement. Under this title, a
religious organization may require that all applicants
and employees conform to the religious tenets of such
organization.

(d) List of Infectious and Communicable Diseases.

(1) In General. The Secretary of Health and Human Services, not later than 6 months after the date of enactment of this Act, shall

(A) review all infectious and communicable diseases which may be transmitted through handling the food supply;

(B) publish a list of infectious and communicable diseases which are transmitted through handling the food supply;

(C) publish the methods by which such diseases are transmitted; and

(D) widely disseminate such information regarding the list of diseases and their modes of transmissability to the general public.

Such list shall be updated annually.

(2) Applications. In any case in which an individual has an infectious or communicable disease that is transmitted to others through the handling of food, that is included on the list developed by the Secretary of Health and Human Services under paragraph (1), and which cannot be eliminated by reasonable accommodation, a covered entity may refuse to assign or continue to assign such individual to a job involving food handling.

(3) Construction. Nothing in this Act shall be construed to preempt, modify, or amend any State, county, or local law, ordinance, or regulation applicable to food han-

dling which is designed to protect the public health from individuals who pose a significant risk to the health or safety of others, which cannot be eliminated by reasonable accommodation, pursuant to the list of infectious or communicable diseases and the modes of transmissability published by the Secretary of Health and Human Services.

Section 104. Illegal Use of Drugs and Alcohol

(a) Qualified Individual with a Disability. For purposes of this title, the term "qualified individual with a disability" shall not include any employee or applicant who is currently engaging in the illegal use of drugs, when the covered entity acts on the basis of such use.

(b) Rules of Construction. Nothing in subsection (a) shall be construed to exclude as a qualified individual with a disability an individual who

(1) has successfully completed a supervised drug rehabilitation program and is no longer engaging in the illegal use of drugs, or has otherwise been rehabilitated successfully and is no longer engaging in such use;

(2) is participating in a supervised rehabilitation program and is no longer engaging in such use; or

(3) is erroneously regarded as engaging in such use, but is not engaging in such use;

except that it shall not be a violation of this Act for a covered entity to adopt or administer reasonable policies or procedures, including but not limited to drug testing, designed to ensure that an individual described in paragraph (1) or (2) is no longer engaging in the illegal use of drugs.

(c) Authority of Covered Entity. A covered entity

(1) may prohibit the illegal use of drugs and the use of alcohol at the workplace by all employees;

(2) may require that employees shall not be under the influence of alcohol or be engaging in the illegal use of drugs at the workplace;

(3) may require that employees behave in conformance with the requirements established under the Drug-Free Workplace Act of 1988;

(4) may hold an employee who engages in the illegal use of drugs or who is an alcoholic to the same qualification standards for employment or job performance and behavior that such entity holds other employees, even if any unsatisfactory performance or behavior is related to the drug use or alcoholism of such employee; and

(5) may, with respect to Federal regulations regarding alcohol and the illegal use of drugs, require that

(A) employees comply with the standards established in such regulations of the Department of Defense, if the employees of the covered entity are employed in an industry subject to such regulations, including complying with regulations (if any) that apply to employment in sensitive positions in such an industry, in the case of employees of the covered entity who are employed in such positions (as defined in the regulations of the Department of Defense);

(B) employees comply with the standards established in such regulations of the Nuclear Regulatory Commission, if the employees of the covered entity are employed in an industry subject to such regulations, including complying with regulations (if any) that apply to employment in sensitive positions in such an industry, in the case of employees of the covered entity who are employed in such positions (as defined in the regulations of the Nuclear Regulatory Commission); and

(C) employees comply with the standards established in such regulations of the Department of Transportation, if the employees of the covered entity are employed in a transportation industry subject to such regulations, including complying with such regulations (if any) that apply to employment in sensitive positions in such an industry, in the case of employees of the covered entity who are employed in such positions (as defined in the regulations of the Department of Transportation).

(d) Drug Testing.

(1) In General. For purposes of this title, a test to determine the illegal use of drugs shall not be considered a medical examination.

(2) Construction. Nothing in this title shall be construed to encourage, prohibit, or authorize the conducting of drug testing for the illegal use of drugs by job

applicants or employees or making employment decisions based on such test results.

(e) Transportation Employees. Nothing in this title shall be construed to encourage, prohibit, restrict, or authorize the otherwise lawful exercise by entities subject to the jurisdiction of the Department of Transportation of authority to

(1) test employees of such entities in, and applicants for, positions involving safety-sensitive duties for the illegal use of drugs and for on-duty impairment by alcohol; and

(2) remove such persons who test positive for illegal use of drugs and on-duty impairment by alcohol pursuant to paragraph (1) from safety-sensitive duties in implementing subsection (c).

Employers are not prohibited from discriminating against a person based on current illegal use of drugs. However, a person who illegally uses drugs, but is discriminated against because of some other disability that is covered under the Act, is still protected against such discrimination. The person is simply not protected against adverse actions taken on the basis of such person's illegal use of drugs.

Section 105. Posting Notices

Every employer, employment agency, labor organization, or joint labor-management committee covered under this title shall post notices in an accessible format to applicants, employees, and members describing the applicable provisions of this Act, in the manner prescribed by section 711 of the Civil Rights Act of 1964.

Section 106. Regulations

Not later than 1 year after the date of enactment of this Act, the Commission shall issue regulations in an accessible format to carry out this title in accordance with subchapter II of chapter 5 of title 5, United States Code.

Section 107. Enforcement

(a) Powers, Remedies, and Procedures. The powers, remedies, and procedures set forth in sections 705, 706, 707, 709, and 710 of the Civil Rights Act of 1964 shall be the powers, remedies, and procedures this title provides to the Commission, to the Attorney General, or to any person alleging discrimination on the basis of disability in violation of any provision of this Act, or regulations promulgated under section 106, concerning employment.

(b) Coordination. The agencies with enforcement authority for actions which allege employment discrimination under this title and under the Rehabilitation Act of 1973 shall develop procedures to ensure that administrative complaints filed under this title and under the Rehabilitation Act of 1973 are dealt with in a manner that avoids duplication of effort and prevents imposition of inconsistent or conflicting standards for the same requirements under this title and the Rehabilitation Act of 1973. The Commission, the Attorney General, and the Office of Federal Contract Compliance Programs shall establish such coordinating mechanisms (similar to provisions contained in the joint regulations promulgated by the Commission and the Attorney General at part 42 of title 28 and part

1691 of title 29, Code of Federal Regulations, and the Memorandum of Understanding between the Commission and the Office of Federal Contract Compliance Programs dated January 16, 1981 in regulations implementing this title and the Rehabilitation Act of 1973 not later than 18 months after the date of enactment of this Act.

Section 108. Effective Date

This title shall become effective 24 months after the date of enactment.

.

Title II - Public Services

Subtitle A
Prohibition Against Discrimination and Other Generally Applicable Provisions

Subtitle B
Actions Applicable to Public Transportation Provided by Public Entities Considered Discriminatory

Part I
Public Transportation Other Than by Aircraft or Certain Rail Operations

Part II
Public Transportation by Intercity and Commuter Rail

TITLE II - PUBLIC SERVICES

Subtitle A - Prohibition Against Discrimination and Other Generally Applicable Provisions

Section 201. Definitions

As used in this title:

(1) Public Entity. The term "public entity" means

  (A) any State or local government;

  (B) any department, agency, special purpose district, or other instrumentality of a State or States or local government; and

  (C) the National Railroad Passenger Corporation, and any commuter authority (as defined in section 103(8) of the Rail Passenger Service Act).

(2) Qualified Individual with a Disability. The term "qualified individual with a disability" means an individual with a disability who, with or without reasonable modifications to rules, policies, or practices, the removal of architectural, communication, or transportation barriers, or the provision of auxiliary aids and services, meets the essential eligibility requirements for the receipt of services or the participation in programs or activities provided by a public entity.

Section 202. Discrimination

Subject to the provisions of this title, no qualified individual with a disability shall, by reason of such disability, be excluded from participation in or be denied the benefits of the services, programs, or activities of a public entity, or be subjected to discrimination by any such entity.

In order to comply with the non-discrimination mandate, it is often necessary to provide training to public employees about disability. For example, persons who have epilepsy, and a variety of other disabilities, are frequently inappropriately arrested and jailed because police officers have not received proper training in the recognition of and aid for seizures. Often, after being arrested, they are deprived of medications while in jail, resulting in further seizures. Such discriminatory treatment based on disability can be avoided by proper training.

The provision of reasonable accommodation is central to the non-discrimination mandate. Courts have recognized that the Rehabilitation Act "mandates significant accommodation for the capabilities and conditions of the handicapped," which may require "substantial amounts of time and money to keep handicapped employees on the payroll."

In determining whether an accommodation would constitute an undue hardship, a number of factors, including the size and budget of the employer are set forth as factors to be considered.

[A] small day-care center might not be required to expend more than a nominal sum, such as that necessary to equip a telephone for use by a secretary with impaired hearing, but a large school district might be required to make available a teacher's aide to a blind applicant for a teaching job. Further, it might be considered reasonable to require a state welfare agency to accommodate a deaf employee by providing an interpreter, while it would consti-

tute an undue hardship to [impose] that requirement on a provider of foster home care services.

[T]he undue hardship determination is flexible, depending on the facts of an individual case. The employer must demonstrate that a reasonable accommodation would impose an undue hardship.

Section 203. Enforcement

The remedies, procedures, and rights set forth in section 505 of the Rehabilitation Act of 1973 shall be the remedies, procedures, and rights this title provides to any person alleging discrimination on the basis of disability in violation of section 202.

Section 204. Regulations

(a) In General. Not later than 1 year after the date of enactment of this Act, the Attorney General shall promulgate regulations in an accessible format that implement this subtitle. Such regulations shall not include any matter within the scope of the authority of the Secretary of Transportation under section 223, 229, or 244.

(b) Relationship to Other Regulations. Except for "program accessibility, existing facilities", and "communications", regulations under subsection (a) shall be consistent with this Act and with the coordination regulations under part 41 of title 28, Code of Federal Regulations (as promulgated by the Department of Health, Education, and Welfare on January 13, 1978), applicable to recipients of Federal financial assistance under section 504 of the Rehabilitation Act of 1973. With respect to "program accessibility, existing facilities", and "communications", such regulations shall be consistent with regulations and analysis as in part 39 of title 28 of the Code of Federal Regulations, applicable to federally conducted activities under such section 504.

(c) Standards. Regulations under subsection (a) shall include standards applicable to facilities and vehicles covered by this subtitle, other than facilities, stations, rail passenger cars, and vehicles covered by subtitle B. Such standards shall be consistent with the minimum guidelines and requirements issued by the Architectural and Transportation Barriers Compliance Board in accordance with section 504(a) of this Act.

Unlike the other titles in this Act, title II does not list all of the forms of discrimination that the title is intended to prohibit. Thus, the purpose of this section is to direct the Attorney General to issue regulations setting forth the forms of discrimination prohibited.

Section 205. Effective Date

(a) General Rule. Except as provided in subsection (b), this subtitle shall become effective 18 months after the date of enactment of this Act.

(b) Exception. Section 204 shall become effective on the date of enactment of this Act.

Subtitle B - Actions Applicable to Public Transportation Provided by Public Entities Considered Discriminatory

Part I - Public Transportation Other Than by Aircraft or Certain Rail Operations

Section 221. Definitions

As used in this part:

(1) Demand Responsive System. The term "demand responsive system" means any system of providing designated public transportation which is not a fixed route system.

(2) Designated Public Transportation. The term "designated public transportation" means transportation (other than public school transportation) by bus, rail, or any other conveyance (other than transportation by aircraft or intercity or commuter rail transportation (as defined in section 241) that provides the general public with general or special service (including charter service) on a regular and continuing basis.

(3) Fixed Route System. The term "fixed route system" means a system of providing designated public transportation on which a vehicle is operated along a prescribed route according to a fixed schedule.

(4) Operates. The term "operates", as used with respect to a fixed route system or demand responsive system, includes operation of such system by a person under a con-

tractual or other arrangement or relationship with a public entity.

(5) Public School Transportation. The term "public school transportation" means transportation by schoolbus vehicles of schoolchildren, personnel, and equipment to and from a public elementary or secondary school and school-related activities.

(6) Secretary. The term "Secretary" means the Secretary of Transportation.

Section 222. Public Entities Operating Fixed Route Systems

(a) Purchase and Lease of New Vehicles. It shall be considered discrimination for purposes of section 202 of this Act and section 504 of the Rehabilitation Act of 1973 for a public entity which operates a fixed route system to purchase or lease a new bus, a new rapid rail vehicle, a new light rail vehicle, or any other new vehicle to be used on such system, if the solicitation for such purchase or lease is made after the 30th day following the effective date of this subsection and if such bus, rail vehicle, or other vehicle is not readily accessible to and usable by individuals with disabilities, including individuals who use wheelchairs.

(b) Purchase and Lease of Used Vehicles. Subject to subsection (c)(1), it shall be considered discrimination for purposes of section 202 of this Act and section 504 of the Rehabilitation Act of 1973 for a public entity which operates a fixed route system to purchase or lease, after the 30th day following the effective date of this subsection, a used vehicle for use on such system unless such entity makes demonstrated good faith efforts to purchase or lease a used vehicle for use on such system that is readily accessible to and usable by individuals with disabilities, including individuals who use wheelchairs.

(c) Remanufactured Vehicles.

(1) General Rule. Except as provided in paragraph (2), it shall be considered discrimination for purposes of section 202 of this Act and section 504 of the Rehabilitation Act of 1973 for a public entity which operates a fixed route system

(A) to remanufacture a vehicle for use on such system so as to extend its usable life for 5 years or more, which remanufacture begins (or for which the solicitation is made) after the 30th day following the effective date of this subsection; or

(B) to purchase or lease for use on such system a remanufactured vehicle which has been remanufactured so as to extend its usable life for 5 years or more, which purchase or lease occurs after such 30th day and during the period in which the usable life is extended;

unless, after remanufacture, the vehicle is, to the maximum extent feasible, readily accessible to and usable by individuals with disabilities, including individuals who use wheelchairs.

(2) Exception for Historic Vehicles.

(A) General Rule. If a public entity operates a fixed route system any segment of which is included on

the National Register of Historic Places and if making a vehicle of historic character to be used solely
on such segment readily accessible to and usable by
individuals with disabilities would significantly alter
the historic character of such vehicle, the public entity only has to make (or to purchase or lease a remanufactured vehicle with) those modifications
which are necessary to meet the requirements of
paragraph (1) and which do not significantly alter
the historic character of such vehicle.

(B) Vehicles of Historic Character Defined by Regulations. For purposes of this paragraph and section
228(b), a vehicle of historic character shall be defined by the regulations issued by the Secretary to
carry out this subsection.

**Section 223. Paratransit as a Complement to Fixed
Route Service**

(a) General Rule. It shall be considered discrimination for
purposes of section 202 of this Act and section 504 of the
Rehabilitation Act of 1973 for a public entity which operates a fixed route system (other than a system which
provides solely commuter bus service) to fail to provide
with respect to the operations of its fixed route system, in
accordance with this section, paratransit and other special
transportation services to individuals with disabilities, including individuals who use wheelchairs, that are sufficient to provide to such individuals a level of service (1)
which is comparable to the level of designated public
transportation services provided to individuals without
disabilities using such system; or (2) in the case of re-
sponse time, which is comparable, to the extent practicable, to the level of designated public transportation serv-

ices provided to individuals without disabilities using such system.

(b) Issuance of Regulations. Not later than 1 year after the effective date of this subsection, the Secretary shall issue final regulations to carry out this section.

(c) Required Contents of Regulations.

(1) Eligible Recipients of Service. The regulations issued under this section shall require each public entity which operates a fixed route system to provide the paratransit and other special transportation services required under this section

(A)(i) to any individual with a disability who is unable, as a result of a physical or mental impairment (including a vision impairment) and without the assistance of another individual (except an operator of a wheelchair lift or other boarding assistance device), to board, ride, or disembark from any vehicle on the system which is readily accessible to and usable by individuals with disabilities;

(ii) to any individual with a disability who needs the assistance of a wheelchair lift or other boarding assistance device (and is able with such assistance) to board, ride, and disembark from any vehicle which is readily accessible to and usable by individuals with disabilities if the individual wants to travel on a route on the system during the hours of operation of the system at a time (or within a reasonable period of such time) when such a vehicle is not being used to provide designated public transportation on the route; and

(iii) to any individual with a disability who has a specific impairment-related condition which prevents such individual from traveling to a boarding location or from a disembarking location on such system;

(B) to one other individual accompanying the individual with the disability; and

(C) to other individuals, in addition to the one individual described in subparagraph (B), accompanying the individual with a disability provided that space for these additional individuals is available on the paratransit vehicle carrying the individual with a disability and that the transportation of such additional individuals will not result in a denial of service to individuals with disabilities.

For purposes of clauses (i) and (ii) of subparagraph (A), boarding or disembarking from a vehicle does not include travel to the boarding location or from the disembarking location.

(2) Service Area. The regulations issued under this section shall require the provision of paratransit and special transportation services required under this section in the service area of each public entity which operates a fixed route system, other than any portion of the service area in which the public entity solely provides commuter bus service.

(3) Service Criteria. Subject to paragraphs (1) and (2), the regulations issued under this section shall establish minimum service criteria for determining the level of services to be required under this section.

(4) Undue Financial Burden Limitation. The regulations issued under this section shall provide that, if the public entity is able to demonstrate to the satisfaction of the Secretary that the provision of paratransit and other special transportation services otherwise required under this section would impose an undue financial burden on the public entity, the public entity, notwithstanding any other provision of this section (other than paragraph (5)), shall only be required to provide such services to the extent that providing such services would not impose such a burden.

(5) Additional Services. The regulations issued under this section shall establish circumstances under which the Secretary may require a public entity to provide, notwithstanding paragraph (4), paratransit and other special transportation services under this section beyond the level of paratransit and other special transportation services which would otherwise be required under paragraph (4).

(6) Public Participation. The regulations issued under this section shall require that each public entity which operates a fixed route system hold a public hearing, provide an opportunity for public comment, and consult with individuals with disabilities in preparing its plan under paragraph (7).

(7) Plans. The regulations issued under this section shall require that each public entity which operates a fixed route system

(A) within 18 months after the effective date of this subsection, submit to the Secretary, and commence implementation of, a plan for providing paratransit and other special transportation services which meets the requirements of this section; and

(B) on an annual basis thereafter, submit to the Secretary, and commence implementation of, a plan for providing such services.

(8) Provision of Services by Others. The regulations issued under this section shall

(A) require that a public entity submitting a plan to the Secretary under this section identify in the plan any person or other public entity which is providing a paratransit or other special transportation service for individuals with disabilities in the service area to which the plan applies;

and

(B) provide that the public entity submitting the plan does not have to provide under the plan such service for individuals with disabilities.

(9) Other Provisions. The regulations issued under this section shall include such other provisions and requirements as the Secretary determines are necessary to carry out the objectives of this section.

(d) Review of Plan.

(1) General Rule. The Secretary shall review a plan submitted under this section for the purpose of determining whether or not such plan meets the requirements of this section, including the regulations issued under this section.

(2) Disapproval. If the Secretary determines that a plan reviewed under this subsection fails to meet the requirements of this section, the Secretary shall disapprove the plan and notify the public entity which submitted the plan of such disapproval and the reasons therefor.

(3) Modification of Disapproved Plan. Not later than 90 days after the date of disapproval of a plan under this subsection, the public entity which submitted the plan shall modify the plan to meet the requirements of this section and shall submit to the Secretary, and commence implementation of, such modified plan.

(e) Discrimination Defined. As used in subsection (a), the term "discrimination" includes

(1) a failure of a public entity to which the regulations issued under this section apply to submit, or commence implementation of, a plan in accordance with subsections (c)(6) and (c)(7);

(2) a failure of such entity to submit, or commence implementation of, a modified plan in accordance with subsection (d)(3);

(3) submission to the Secretary of a modified plan under subsection (d)(3) which does not meet the requirements of this section; or

(4) a failure of such entity to provide paratransit or other special transportation services in accordance with the plan or modified plan the public entity submitted to the Secretary under this section.

(f) Statutory Construction. Nothing in this section shall be construed as preventing a public entity

(1) from providing paratransit or other special transportation services at a level which is greater than the level of such services which are required by this section,

(2) from providing paratransit or other special transportation services in addition to those paratransit and special transportation services required by this section, or

(3) from providing such services to individuals in addition to those individuals to whom such services are required to be provided by this section.

Section 224. Public Entity Operating A Demand Responsive System

If a public entity operates a demand responsive system, it shall be considered discrimination, for purposes of section 202 of this Act and section 504 of the Rehabilitation Act of 1973, for such entity to purchase or lease a new vehicle for use on such system, for which a solicitation is made after the 30th day following the effective date of this section, that is not readily accessible to and usable by individuals with disabilities, including individuals who use wheelchairs, unless such system, when viewed in its entirety, provides a level of service to such individuals equivalent to the level of service such system provides to individuals without disabilities.

Section 225. Temporary Relief Where Lifts Are Unavailable

(a) Granting. With respect to the purchase of new buses, a public entity may apply for, and the Secretary may temporarily relieve such public entity from the obligation under section 222(a) or 224 to purchase new buses that are readily accessible to and usable by individuals with disabilities if such public entity demonstrates to the satisfaction of the Secretary

(1) that the initial solicitation for new buses made by the public entity specified that all new buses were to be lift-equipped and were to be otherwise accessible to and usable by individuals with disabilities;

(2) the unavailability from any qualified manufacturer of hydraulic, electromechanical, or other lifts for such new buses;

(3) that the public entity seeking temporary relief has made good faith efforts to locate a qualified manufacturer to supply the lifts to the manufacturer of such buses in sufficient time to comply with such solicitation; and

(4) that any further delay in purchasing new buses necessary to obtain such lifts would significantly impair transportation services in the community served by the public entity.

(b) Duration and Notice to Congress. Any relief granted under subsection (a) shall be limited in duration by a specified date, and the appropriate committees of Congress shall be notified of any such relief granted.

(c) Fraudulent Application. If, at any time, the Secretary has reasonable cause to believe that any relief granted under subsection (a) was fraudulently applied for, the Secretary shall

(1) cancel such relief if such relief is still in effect; and

(2) take such other action as the Secretary considers appropriate.

Section 226. New Facilities

For purposes of section 202 of this Act and section 504 of the Rehabilitation Act of 1973, it shall be considered discrimination for a public entity to construct a new facility to be used in the provision of designated public transportation services unless such facility is readily accessible to and usable by individuals with disabilities, including individuals who use wheelchairs.

Section 227. Alterations of Existing Facilities

(a) General Rule. With respect to alterations of an existing facility or part thereof used in the provision of designated public transportation services that affect or could affect the usability of the facility or part thereof, it shall be considered discrimination, for purposes of section 202 of this Act and section 504 of the Rehabilitation Act of 1973, for a public entity to fail to make such alterations (or to ensure that the alterations are made) in such a manner that, to the maximum extent feasible, the altered portions of the facility are readily accessible to and usable by individuals with disabilities, including individuals who use wheelchairs, upon the completion of such alterations. Where the public entity is undertaking an alteration that affects or could affect usability of or access to an area of the facility containing a primary function, the entity shall also make the alterations in such a manner that, to the maximum extent feasible, the path of travel to the altered area and the bathrooms, telephones, and drinking fountains serving the altered area, are readily accessible to and usable by individuals with disabilities, including individuals who use wheelchairs, upon completion of such alterations, where such alterations to the path of travel or the bathrooms, telephones, and drinking fountains serving the altered area are not disproportionate to the overall alterations in terms of cost and scope (as determined under criteria established by the Attorney General).

(b) Special Rule for Stations.

(1) General Rule. For purposes of section 202 of this Act and section 504 of the Rehabilitation Act of 1973, it shall be considered discrimination for a public entity that provides designated public transportation to fail, in accordance with the provisions of this subsection, to make key stations (as determined under criteria established by the Secretary by regulation) in rapid rail and light rail systems readily accessible to and usable by individuals with disabilities, including individuals who use wheelchairs.

(2) Rapid Rail and Light Rail Key Stations.

(A) Accessibility. Except as otherwise provided in this paragraph, all key stations (as determined under criteria established by the Secretary by regulation) in rapid rail and light rail systems shall be made readily accessible to and usable by individuals with disabilities, including individuals who use wheelchairs, as soon as practicable but in no event later than the last day of the 3-year period beginning on the effective date of this paragraph.

(B) Extension for Extraordinarily Expensive Structural Changes. The Secretary may extend the 3-year period under subparagraph (A) up to a 30-year period for key stations in a rapid rail or light rail system which stations need extraordinarily expensive structural changes to, or replacement of, existing facilities; except that by the last day of the 20th year following the date of the enactment of this Act at least 2/3 of such key stations must be readily accessible to and usable by individuals with disabilities.

(3) Plans and Milestones. The Secretary shall require the appropriate public entity to develop and submit to the Secretary a plan for compliance with this subsection

(A) that reflects consultation with individuals with disabilities affected by such plan and the results of a public hearing and public comments on such plan, and

(B) that establishes milestones for achievement of the requirements of this subsection.

Section 228. Public Transportation Programs and Activities in Existing Facilities and One Car Per Train Rule

(a) Public Transportation Programs and Activities in Existing Facilities.

(1) In General. With respect to existing facilities used in the provision of designated public transportation services, it shall be considered discrimination, for purposes of section 202 of this Act and section 504 of the Rehabilitation Act of 1973, for a public entity to fail to operate a designated public transportation program or activity conducted in such facilities so that, when viewed in the entirety, the program or activity is readily accessible to and usable by individuals with disabilities.

(2) Exception. Paragraph (1) shall not require a public entity to make structural changes to existing facilities in order to make such facilities accessible to individuals who use wheelchairs, unless and to the extent required by section 227(a) (relating to alterations) or section 227(b) (relating to key stations).

(3) Utilization. Paragraph (1) shall not require a public entity to which paragraph (2) applies, to provide to individuals who use wheelchairs services made available to the general public at such facilities when such individuals could not utilize or benefit from such services provided at such facilities.

(b) One Car per Train Rule.

(1) General Rule. Subject to paragraph (2), with respect to 2 or more vehicles operated as a train by a light or rapid rail system, for purposes of section 202 of this Act and section 504 of the Rehabilitation Act of 1973, it shall be considered discrimination for a public entity to fail to have at least 1 vehicle per train that is accessible to individuals with disabilities, including individuals who use wheelchairs, as soon as practicable but in

no event later than the last day of the 5-year period beginning on the effective date of this section.

(2) Historic Trains. In order to comply with paragraph (1) with respect to the remanufacture of a vehicle of historic character which is to be used on a segment of a light or rapid rail system which is included on the National Register of Historic Places, if making such vehicle readily accessible to and usable by individuals with disabilities would significantly alter the historic character of such vehicle, the public entity which operates such system only has to make (or to purchase or lease a remanufactured vehicle with) those modifications which are necessary to meet the requirements of section 222(c)(1) and which do not significantly alter the historic character of such vehicle.

Section 229. Regulations

(a) In General. Not later than 1 year after the date of enactment of this Act, the Secretary of Transportation shall issue regulations, in an accessible format, necessary for carrying out this part (other than section 223).

(b) Standards. The regulations issued under this section and section 223 shall include standards applicable to facilities and vehicles covered by this subtitle. The standards shall be consistent with the minimum guidelines and requirements issued by the Architectural and Transportation Barriers Compliance Board in accordance with section 504 of this Act.

Section 230. Interim Accessibility Requirements

If final regulations have not been issued pursuant to section 229, for new construction or alterations for which a valid and appropriate State or local building permit is obtained prior to the issuance of final regulations under such section, and for which the construction or alteration authorized by such permit begins within one year of the receipt of such permit and is completed under the terms of such permit, compliance with the Uniform Federal Accessibility Standards in effect at the time the building permit is issued shall suffice to satisfy the requirement that facilities be readily accessible to and usable by persons with disabilities as required under sections 226 and 227, except that, if such final regulations have not been issued one year after the Architectural and Transportation Barriers Compliance Board has issued the supplemental minimum guidelines required under section 504(a) of this Act, compliance with such supplemental minimum guidelines shall be necessary to satisfy the requirement that facilities be readily accessible to and usable by persons with disabilities prior to issuance of the final regulations.

Section 231. Effective Date

(a) General Rule. Except as provided in subsection (b), this part shall become effective 18 months after the date of enactment of this Act.

(b) Exception. Sections 222, 223 (other than subsection (a)), 224, 225, 227(b), 228(b), and 229 shall become effective on the date of enactment of this Act.

Part II - Public Transportation by Intercity and Commuter Rail

Section 241. Definitions

As used in this part:

(1) Commuter Authority. The term "commuter authority" has the meaning given such term in section 103(8) of the Rail Passenger Service Act.

(2) Commuter Rail Transportation. The term "commuter rail transportation" has the meaning given the term "commuter service" in section 103(9) of the Rail Passenger Service Act.

(3) Intercity Rail Transportation. The term "intercity rail transportation" means transportation provided by the National Railroad Passenger Corporation.

(4) Rail Passenger Car. The term "rail passenger car" means, with respect to intercity rail transportation, single-level and bi-level coach cars, single level and bi-level dining cars, single-level and bi-level sleeping cars, single-level and bi-level lounge cars, and food service cars.

(5) Responsible Person. The term "responsible person" means

(A) in the case of a station more than 50 percent of which is owned by a public entity, such public entity;

(B) in the case of a station more than 50 percent of which is owned by a private party, the persons providing intercity or commuter rail transportation to such station, as allocated on an equitable basis by regulation by the Secretary of Transportation; and

(C) in a case where no party owns more than 50 percent of a station, the persons providing intercity or commuter rail transportation to such station and the owners of the station, other than private party owners, as allocated on an equitable basis by regulation by the Secretary of Transportation.

(6) Station. The term "station" means the portion of a property located appurtenant to a right-of-way on which intercity or commuter rail transportation is operated, where such portion is used by the general public and is related to the provision of such transportation, including passenger platforms, designated waiting areas, ticketing areas, restrooms, and, where a public entity providing rail transportation owns the property, concession areas, to the extent that such public entity exercises control over the selection, design, construction, or alteration of the property, but such term does not include flag stops.

Section 242. Intercity and Commuter Rail Actions Considered Discriminatory

(a) Intercity Rail Transportation.

(1) One Car per Train Rule. It shall be considered discrimination for purposes of section 202 of this Act and section 504 of the Rehabilitation Act of 1973 for a person who provides intercity rail transportation to fail to have at least one passenger car per train that is readily accessible to and usable by individuals with disabilities, including individuals who use wheelchairs, in accordance with regulations issued under section

244, as soon as practicable, but in no event later than 5 years after the date of enactment of this Act.

(2) New Intercity Cars.

(A) General Rule. Except as otherwise provided in this subsection with respect to individuals who use wheelchairs, it shall be considered discrimination for purposes of section 202 of this Act and section 504 of the Rehabilitation Act of 1973 for a person to purchase or lease any new rail passenger cars for use in intercity rail transportation, and for which a solicitation is made later than 30 days after the effective date of this section, unless all such rail cars are readily accessible to and usable by individuals with disabilities, including individuals who use wheelchairs, as prescribed by the Secretary of Transportation in regulations issued under section 244.

(B) Special Rule for Single-Level Passenger Coaches for Individuals Who Use Wheelchairs. Single-level passenger coaches shall be required to

(i) be able to be entered by an individual who uses a wheelchair;

(ii) have space to park and secure a wheelchair;

(iii) have a seat to which a passenger in a wheelchair can transfer, and a space to fold and store such passenger's wheelchair; and

(iv) have a restroom usable by an individual who uses a wheelchair, only to the extent provided in paragraph (3).

(C) Special Rule for Single-Level Dining Cars for Individuals Who Use Wheelchairs. Single-level dining cars shall not be required to

(i) be able to be entered from the station platform by an individual who uses a wheelchair; or

(ii) have a restroom usable by an individual who uses a wheelchair if no restroom is provided in such car for any passenger.

(D) Special Rule for Bi-Level Dining Cars for Individuals Who Use Wheelchairs. Bi-level dining cars shall not be required to

(i) be able to be entered by an individual who uses a wheelchair;

(ii) have space to park and secure a wheelchair;

(iii) have a seat to which a passenger in a wheelchair can transfer, or a space to fold and store such passenger's wheelchair; or

(iv) have a restroom usable by an individual who uses a wheelchair.

(3) Accessibility of Single-level Coaches.

(A) General Rule. It shall be considered discrimination for purposes of section 202 of this Act and section 504 of the Rehabilitation Act of 1973 for a person who provides intercity rail transportation to fail to have on each train which includes one or more single-level rail passenger coaches

(i) a number of spaces

(I) to park and secure wheelchairs (to accommodate individuals who wish to remain in their wheelchairs) equal to not less than one-half of the number of single-level rail passenger coaches in such train; and

(II) to fold and store wheelchairs (to accommodate individuals who wish to transfer to coach seats) equal to not less than one-half of the number of single-level rail passenger coaches in such train,

as soon as practicable, but in no event later than 5 years after the date of enactment of this Act; and

(ii) a number of spaces

(I) to park and secure wheelchairs (to accommodate individuals who wish to remain in their wheelchairs) equal to not less than the total number of single-level rail passenger coaches in such train; and

(II) to fold and store wheelchairs (to accommodate individuals who wish to transfer to coach seats) equal to not less than the total number of single-level rail passenger coaches in such train,

as soon as practicable, but in no event later than 10 years after the date of enactment of this Act.

(B) Location. Spaces required by subparagraph (A) shall be located in single-level rail passenger coaches or food service cars.

(C) Limitation. Of the number of spaces required on a train by subparagraph (A), not more than two spaces to park and secure wheelchairs nor more than two spaces to fold and store wheelchairs shall be located in any one coach or food service car.

(D) Other Accessibility Features. Single-level rail passenger coaches and food service cars on which the spaces required by subparagraph (A) are located shall have a restroom usable by an individual who uses a wheelchair and shall be able to be entered from the station platform by an individual who uses a wheelchair.

(4) Food Service.

(A) Single-level Dining Cars. On any train in which a single-level dining car is used to provide food service

(i) if such single-level dining car was purchased after the date of enactment of this Act, table service in such car shall be provided to a passenger who uses a wheelchair if

(I) the car adjacent to the end of the dining car through which a wheelchair may enter is itself accessible to a wheelchair;

(II) such passenger can exit to the platform from the car such passenger occupies, move down the platform, and enter the adjacent accessible car described in subclause (I) without the necessity of the train being moved within the station; and

(III) space to park and secure a wheelchair is available in the dining car at the time such passenger wishes to eat (if such passenger wishes to remain in a wheelchair), or space to store and fold a wheelchair is available in the dining car at the time such passenger wishes to eat (if such passenger wishes to transfer to a dining car seat); and

(ii) appropriate auxiliary aids and services, including a hard surface on which to eat, shall be provided to ensure that other equivalent food service is available to individuals with disabilities, including individuals who use wheelchairs, and to passengers traveling with such individuals.

Unless not practicable, a person providing intercity rail transportation shall place an accessible car adjacent to the end of a dining car described in clause (i) through which an individual who uses a wheelchair may enter.

(B) Bi-level Dining Cars. On any train in which a bi-level dining car is used to provide food service

(i) if such train includes a bi-level lounge car purchased after the date of enactment of this Act, table service in such lounge car shall be provided to individuals who use wheelchairs and to other passengers; and

(ii) appropriate auxiliary aids and services, including a hard surface on which to eat, shall be provided to ensure that other equivalent food service is available to individuals with disabilities, including individuals who use wheelchairs, and to passengers traveling with such individuals.

(b) Commuter Rail Transportation.

(1) One Car per Train Rule. It shall be considered discrimination for purposes of section 202 of this Act and section 504 of the Rehabilitation Act of 1973 for a person who provides commuter rail transportation to fail to have at least one passenger car per train that is readily accessible to and usable by individuals with disabilities, including individuals who use wheelchairs, in accordance with regulations issued under section 244, as soon as practicable, but in no event later than 5 years after the date of enactment of this Act.

(2) New Commuter Rail Cars.

(A) General Rule. It shall be considered discrimination for purposes of section 202 of this Act and section 504 of the Rehabilitation Act of 1973 for a person to purchase or lease any new rail passenger cars for use in commuter rail transportation, and for which a solicitation is made later than 30 days after the effective date of this section, unless all such rail cars are readily accessible to and usable by individuals with disabilities, including individuals who use wheelchairs, as prescribed by the Secretary of Transportation in regulations issued under section 244.

(B) Accessibility. For purposes of section 202 of this Act and section 504 of the Rehabilitation Act of 1973, a requirement that a rail passenger car used in commuter rail transportation be accessible to or readily accessible to and usable by individuals with disabilities, including individuals who use wheelchairs, shall not be construed to require

(i) a restroom usable by an individual who uses a wheelchair if no restroom is provided in such car for any passenger;

(ii) space to fold and store a wheelchair; or

(iii) a seat to which a passenger who uses a wheelchair can transfer.

(c) Used Rail Cars. It shall be considered discrimination for purposes of section 202 of this Act and Section 504 of the Rehabilitation Act of 1973 for a person to purchase or lease a used rail passenger car for use in intercity or commuter rail transportation, unless such person makes demonstrated good faith efforts to purchase or lease a used rail car that is readily accessible to and usable by individuals with disabilities, including individuals who use wheelchairs, as prescribed by the Secretary of Transportation in regulations issued under section 244.

(d) Remanufactured Rail Cars.

(1) Remanufacturing. It shall be considered discrimination for purposes of section 202 of this Act and section 504 of the Rehabilitation Act of 1973 for a person to remanufacture a rail passenger car for use in intercity or commuter rail transportation so as to extend its usa-

ble life for 10 years or more, unless the rail car, to the maximum extent feasible, is made readily accessible to and usable by individuals with disabilities, including individuals who use wheelchairs, as prescribed by the Secretary of Transportation in regulations issued under section 244.

(2) Purchase or Lease. It shall be considered discrimination for purposes of section 202 of this Act and section 504 of the Rehabilitation Act of 1973 for a person to purchase or lease a remanufactured rail passenger car for use in intercity or commuter rail transportation unless such car was remanufactured in accordance with paragraph (1).

(e) Stations.

(1) New Stations. It shall be considered discrimination for purposes of section 202 of this Act and section 504 of the Rehabilitation Act of 1973 for a person to build a new station for use in intercity or commuter rail transportation that is not readily accessible to and usable by individuals with disabilities, including individuals who use wheelchairs, as prescribed by the Secretary of Transportation in regulations issued under section 244.

(2) Existing Stations.

(A) Failure to Make Readily Accessible.

(i) General Rule. It shall be considered discrimination for purposes of section 202 of this Act and section 504 of the Rehabilitation Act of 1973 for a responsible person to fail to make existing stations in the intercity rail transportation system, and existing key stations in commuter rail transportation systems, readily accessible to and usable by individuals with disabilities, including individuals who use wheelchairs, as prescribed by the Secretary of Transportation in regulations issued under section 244.

(ii) Period for Compliance.

 (I) Intercity Rail. All stations in the intercity rail transportation system shall be made readily accessible to and usable by individuals with disabilities, including individuals who use wheelchairs, as soon as practicable, but in no event later than 20 years after the date of enactment of this Act.

 (II) Commuter Rail. Key stations in commuter rail transportation systems shall be made readily accessible to and usable by individuals with disabilities, including individuals who use wheelchairs, as soon as practicable but in no event later than 3 years after the date of enactment of this Act, except that the time limit may be extended by the Secretary of Transportation up to 20 years after the date of enactment of this Act in a case where the raising of the entire passenger platform is the only means available of attaining accessibility or where other extraordinarily expensive structural changes are necessary to attain accessibility.

(iii) Designation of Key Stations. Each commuter authority shall designate the key stations in its commuter rail transportation system, in consultation with individuals with disabilities and organizations representing such individuals, taking into consideration such factors as high ridership and whether such station serves as a transfer or feeder station. Before the final designation of key stations under this clause, a commuter authority shall hold a public hearing.

(iv) Plans and Milestones. The Secretary of Transportation shall require the appropriate person to develop a plan for carrying out this subparagraph that reflects consultation with individuals with disabilities affected by such plan and that establishes milestones for achievement of the requirements of this subparagraph.

(B) Requirement When Making Alterations.

(i) General Rule. It shall be considered discrimination, for purposes of section 202 of this Act and section 504 of the Rehabilitation Act of 1973, with respect to alterations of an existing station or part thereof in the intercity or commuter rail transportation systems that affect or could affect the usability of the station or part thereof, for the responsible person, owner, or person in control of the station to fail to make the alterations in such a manner that, to the maximum extent feasible, the altered portions of the station are readily accessible to and usable by individuals with disabilities, including individuals who use wheelchairs, upon completion of such alterations.

(ii) Alterations to a Primary Function Area. It shall be considered discrimination, for purposes of section 202 of this Act and section 504 of the Rehabilitation Act of 1973, with respect to alterations that affect or could affect the usability of or access to an area of the station containing a primary function, for the responsible person, owner, or person in control of the station to fail to make the alterations in such a manner that, to the maximum extent feasible, the path of travel to the altered area, and the bathrooms, telephones, and drinking fountains serving the altered area, are readily accessible to and usable by individuals with disabilities, including individuals who use wheelchairs, upon completion of such alterations, where such alterations to the path of travel or the bathrooms, telephones, and drinking fountains serving the altered area are not disproportionate to the overall alterations in terms of cost and scope (as determined under criteria established by the Attorney General).

(C) Required Cooperation. It shall be considered discrimination for purposes of section 202 of this Act and section 504 of the Rehabilitation Act of 1973 for an owner, or person in control, of a station governed by subparagraph (A) or (B) to fail to provide reasonable cooperation to a responsible person with respect to such station in that responsible person's efforts to comply with such subparagraph. An owner, or person in control, of a station shall be liable to a responsible person for any failure to provide reasonable cooperation as required by this subparagraph. Failure to receive reasonable cooperation re-

quired by this subparagraph shall not be a defense
to a claim of discrimination under this Act.

Section 243. Conformance of Accessibility Standards

Accessibility standards included in regulations issued under this part shall be consistent with the minimum guidelines issued by the Architectural and Transportation Barriers Compliance Board under section 504(a) of this Act.

Section 244. Regulations

Not later than 1 year after the date of enactment of this
Act, the Secretary of Transportation shall issue regulations, in an accessible format, necessary for carrying out
this part.

Section 245. Interim Accessibility Requirements

(a) Stations. If final regulations have not been issued pursuant to section 244, for new construction or alterations
for which a valid and appropriate State or local building
permit is obtained prior to the issuance of final regulations under such section, and for which the construction
or alteration authorized by such permit begins within one
year of the receipt of such permit and is completed under
the terms of such permit, compliance with the Uniform
Federal Accessibility Standards in effect at the time the
building permit is issued shall suffice to satisfy the requirement that stations be readily accessible to and usable
by persons with disabilities as required under section
242(e), except that, if such final regulations have not been
issued one year after the Architectural and Transportation

minimum guidelines required under section 504(a) of this Act, compliance with such supplemental minimum guidelines shall be necessary to satisfy the requirement that stations be readily accessible to and usable by persons with disabilities prior to issuance of the final regulations.

(b) Rail Passenger Cars. If final regulations have not been issued pursuant to section 244, a person shall be considered to have complied with the requirements of section 242(a) through (d) that a rail passenger car be readily accessible to and usable by individuals with disabilities, if the design for such car complies with the laws and regulations (including the Minimum Guidelines and Requirements for Accessible Design and such supplemental minimum guidelines as are issued under section 504(a) of this Act) governing accessibility of such cars, to the extent that such laws and regulations are not inconsistent with this part and are in effect at the time such design is substantially completed.

Section 246. Effective Date

(a) General Rule. Except as provided in subsection (b), this part shall become effective 18 months after the date of enactment of this Act.

(b) Exception. Sections 242 and 244 shall become effective on the date of enactment of this Act.

Title III
Public Accommodations and Services Operated by Private Entities

TITLE III - PUBLIC ACCOMMODATIONS AND SERVICES OPERATED BY PRIVATE ENTITIES

Section 301. Definitions

As used in this title:

(1) Commerce. The term "commerce" means travel, trade, traffic, commerce, transportation, or communication

(A) among the several States;

(B) between any foreign country or any territory or possession and any State; or

(C) between points in the same State but through another State or foreign country.

(2) Commercial Facilities. The term "commercial facilities" means facilities

(A) that are intended for nonresidential use; and

(B) whose operations will affect commerce.

Such term shall not include railroad locomotives, railroad freight cars, railroad cabooses, railroad cars described in section 242 or covered under this title, railroad rights-of-way, or facilities that are covered or expressly exempted from coverage under the Fair Housing Act of 1968.

(3) Demand Responsive System. The term "demand responsive system" means any system of providing transportation of individuals by a vehicle, other than a system which is a fixed route system.

(4) Fixed Route System. The term "fixed route system" means a system of providing transportation of individuals (other than by aircraft) on which a vehicle is operated along a prescribed route according to a fixed schedule.

(5) Over-the-Road Bus. The term "over-the-road" bus" means a bus characterized by an elevated passenger deck located over a baggage compartment.

(6) Private Entity. The term "private entity" means any entity other than a public entity (as defined in section 201(1)).

(7) Public Accommodation. The following private entities are considered public accommodations for purposes of this title, if the operations of such entities affect commerce

(A) an inn, hotel, motel, or other place of lodging, except for an establishment located within a building that contains not more than five rooms for rent or hire and that is actually occupied by the proprietor of such establishment as the residence of such proprietor;

(B) a restaurant, bar, or other establishment serving food or drink;

(C) a motion picture house, theater, concert hall, stadium, or other place of exhibition or entertainment;

(D) an auditorium, convention center, lecture hall, or other place of public gathering;

(E) a bakery, grocery store, clothing store, hardware store, shopping center, or other sales or rental establishment;

(F) a laundromat, dry-cleaner, bank, barber shop, beauty shop, travel service, shoe repair service, funeral parlor, gas station, office of an accountant or lawyer, pharmacy, insurance office, professional office of a health care provider, hospital, or other service establishment;

(G) a terminal, depot, or other station used for specified public transportation;

(H) a museum, library, gallery, or other place of public display or collection;

(I) a park, zoo, amusement park, or other place of recreation;

(J) a nursery, elementary, secondary, undergraduate, or postgraduate private school, or other place of education;

(K) a day care center, senior citizen center, homeless shelter, food bank, adoption agency, or other social service center establishment; and

(L) a gymnasium, health spa, bowling alley, golf course, or other place of exercise or recreation.

These 12 listed categories are exhaustive. However, within each category, the bill lists only a number of examples. For example, under category (E), the bill lists "a bakery, grocery store, clothing store, hardware store, shopping center, or other sales or rental establishment."

This list is only a representative sample of the types of entities covered under this category. Other retail or wholesale establishments selling or renting items, such as a book store, videotape rental store, or pet store, would be a public accommodation under this category.

A person alleging discrimination does not have to prove that the entity being charged with discrimination is similar to the examples listed in the definition. Rather, the person must show that the entity falls within the overall category. For example, it is not necessary to show that a jewelry store is like a clothing store. It is sufficient that the jewelry store sells items to the public.

Entities not falling under one of these categories, or not privately operated, or not affecting commerce, are not considered to be public accommodations. Entities that are not public accommodations may be commercial facilities and subject to the requirements of Section 303. Entities operated by governments are not covered by this title, but are covered by other titles of this bill or other federal laws. The fact that a private entity receives funds from federal, state, or local governments would not remove it from coverage under this title.

Both the public accommodation facility and the programs and services offered by the public accommodation cannot discriminate against individuals with disabilities. As discussed below, there is an obligation not to discriminate in programs and services provided by the public accommodation, to remove barriers in existing facilities, and to make new and altered facilities accessible and usable. It is not sufficient to only make facilities accessible and usable; this title prohibits, as well, discrimination in the provision of programs and activities conducted by the public accommodation.

(8) Rail and Railroad. The terms "rail" and "railroad" have the meaning given the term "railroad" in section 202(e) of the Federal Railroad Safety Act of 1970.

(9) Readily Achievable. The term "readily achievable" means easily accomplishable and able to be carried out without much difficulty or expense. In determining whether an action is readily achievable, factors to be considered include

(A) the nature and cost of the action needed under this Act;

(B) the overall financial resources of the facility or facilities involved in the action; the number of persons employed at such facility; the effect on expenses and resources, or the impact otherwise of such action upon the operation of the facility;

(C) the overall financial resources of the covered entity; the overall size of the business of a covered entity with respect to the number of its employees; the number, type, and location of its facilities; and

(D) the type of operation or operations of the covered entity, including the composition, structure, and functions of the workforce of such entity; the geographic separateness, administrative or fiscal relationship of the facility or facilities in question to the covered entity.

Unlike many other terms used in this bill, this is a new term that was not part of earlier civil rights laws, such as the Civil Rights Act of 1964, the Rehabilitation Act of 1973, or their implementing regulations.

The definition provides factors to be considered in making a determination of what is readily achievable in a particular case.

(10) Specified Public Transportation. The term "specified public transportation" means transportation by bus, rail, or any other conveyance (other than by aircraft) that provides the general public with general or special service (including charter service) on a regular and continuing basis.

(11) Vehicle. The term "vehicle" does not include a rail passenger car, railroad locomotive, railroad freight car, railroad caboose, or a railroad car described in section 242 or covered under this title.

Section 302. Prohibition of Discrimination by Public Accommodations

(a) General Rule. No individual shall be discriminated against on the basis of disability in the full and equal enjoyment of the goods, services, facilities, privileges, advantages, or accommodations of any place of public accommodation by any person who owns, leases (or leases to), or operates a place of public accommodation.

Full and equal enjoyment means the right to participate and to have an equal opportunity to obtain the same results as others. It does not mean that an individual with a disability must achieve an identical result or level of achievement as persons without a disability. For example, an exercise class cannot exclude a person who uses a wheelchair because he or she cannot do all of the exercises and derive the same result from the class as persons without a disability.

[I]f an office building contains a doctor's office, both the owner of the building and the doctor's office are required to make readily achievable alterations. It simply makes no practical sense to require the individual public accommodation, a doctor's office for example, to make readily achievable changes to the public accommodation without requiring the owner to make readily achievable changes to the primary entrance to the building.

Similarly, a doorman or guard to an office building containing public accommodations would be required, if requested, to show a person who is blind to the elevator or to write a note to a person who is deaf regarding the floor number of a particular office.

[I]f the corporate headquarters for a chain of restaurants designs all new restaurants to contain barriers to access, an injunction could be brought against the corporation to enjoin the inaccessible new construction.

(b) Construction.

   (1) General prohibition.

     (A) Activities.

       (i) Denial of Participation. It shall be discriminatory to subject an individual or class of individuals on the basis of a disability or disabilities of such individual or class, directly, or through contractual, licensing, or other arrangements, to a denial of the opportunity of the individual or class to participate in or benefit from the goods, services, facilities, privileges, advantages, or accommodations of an entity.

(ii) Participation in Unequal Benefit. It shall be discriminatory to afford an individual or class of individuals, on the basis of a disability or disabilities of such individual or class, directly, or through contractual, licensing, or other arrangements with the opportunity to participate in or benefit from a good, service, facility, privilege, advantage, or accommodation that is not equal to that afforded to other individuals.

(iii) Separate Benefit. It shall be discriminatory to provide an individual or class of individuals, on the basis of a disability or disabilities of such individual or class, directly, or through contractual, licensing, or other arrangements with a good, service, facility, privilege, advantage, or accommodation that is different or separate from that provided to other individuals, unless such action is necessary to provide the individual or class of individuals with a good, service, facility, privilege, advantage, or accommodation, or other opportunity that is as effective as that provided to others.

(iv) Individual or Class of Individuals. For purposes of clauses (i) through (iii) of this subparagraph, the term "individual or class of individuals" refers to the clients or customers of the covered public accommodation that enters into the contractual, licensing or other arrangement.

(B) Integrated Settings. Goods, services, facilities, privileges, advantages, and accommodations shall be afforded to an individual with a disability in the most integrated setting appropriate to the needs of the individual.

Integration is fundamental to the purposes of the ADA. Provision of segregated accommodations and services relegate persons with disabilities to second-class citizen status. For example, it would be a violation of this provision to require persons with disabilities to eat in the back room of a restaurant or to refuse to allow a person with a disability the full use of a health spa because of stereotypes about the person's ability to participate.

For example, it would also be a violation of this Act to segregate seating for persons using wheelchairs to the back of auditoriums or theaters. In addition to providing inferior seating, the patron in a wheelchair may be forced to separate from family or friends during a performance.

At times segregated seating is simply the result of thoughtlessness and indifference. At other times, safety concerns are raised, such as requiring patrons to sit near theater exits because of perceived hazards in case of fire. The purported safety hazard is largely based on inaccurate assumptions and myths about the ability of people with disabilities to get around in such circumstances. People who use wheelchairs vary greatly, as does the general public, in their individual ability to move quickly or slowly.

*A balance between the safety interest and the need
to preserve a choice of seating for movie patrons
who use wheelchairs has already been accomplished
under existing federal accessibility standards that
have applied since 1984 to theaters, auditoriums and
other places of assembly constructed with federal
funds.   These standards provide that wheelchair
seating areas must be "dispersed throughout the seating area" and "located to provide lines of sight comparable to those for all viewing areas."   Wheelchair
areas are not restricted to areas near an exit, but can
be located in various parts of the theater so long as
they "adjoin an accessible route that also serves as a
means of egress in case of emergency."*

*The availability of a choice of seating is critical to
assure that patrons with disabilities are not segregated from family or friends.   New construction must
provide a variety of seating options.   In existing
theaters, efforts should be made to increase seating
options where readily achievable.   If removal of
seats is not readily achievable, the theater must, at a
minimum, modify rules and procedures to allow a
non-disabled companion to sit with a person who
uses a wheelchair, by providing, for example, a fold-
ing chair.   Seating should also be available in the
front of the audience for persons with hearing and
vision impairments, including those who use wheelchairs.*

(C) Opportunity to Participate. Notwithstanding the
existence of separate or different programs or activities provided in accordance with this section, an individual with a disability shall not be denied the op-

portunity to participate in such programs or activities that are not separate or different.

It is critical that the existence of separate specialized services never be used as a justification for exclusion from programs that are not separate or different. For example, the existence of a special art program for persons who are developmentally disabled must not be used as a reason to reject an individual who is retarded from the regular art class if that person prefers to participate in that class. This provision does not require changes in the regular method of instruction that are not required under Sections 302(b)(2)(A)(ii) and (iii).

(D) Administrative Methods. An individual or entity shall not, directly or through contractual or other arrangements, utilize standards or criteria or methods of administration

(i) that have the effect of discriminating on the basis of disability; or

(ii) that perpetuate the discrimination of others who are subject to common administrative control.

(E) Association. It shall be discriminatory to exclude or otherwise deny equal goods, services, facilities, privileges, advantages, accommodations, or other opportunities to an individual or entity because of the known disability of an individual with whom the individual or entity is known to have a relationship or association.

The term "entity" is included in this section because,
at times entities that provide services to, or are oth-
erwise associated with persons with disabilities, are
subjected to discrimination.

The general prohibitions set forth in Section
302(b)(1) are patterned after provisions contained
in other civil rights laws protecting women and min-
orities. In order to provide effective protections for
persons with disabilities, however, additional specific
prohibitions are provided in this section. These spe-
cific provisions, including the limitations contained
within them, control over the general provision to
the extent that [there] is any conflict.

(2) Specific prohibitions.

(A) Discrimination. For purposes of subsection (a),
discrimination includes

(i) the imposition or application of eligibility
criteria that screen out or tend to screen out an
individual with a disability or any class of individuals with disabilities from fully and equally
enjoying any goods, services, facilities, privileges,
advantages, or accommodations, unless such criteria can be shown to be necessary for the provision of the goods, services, facilities, privileges,
advantages, or accommodations being offered;

[I]t would be illegal to require all customers to
present a driver's license in order to purchase
merchandise, because this would screen out per-
sons with disabilities who do not drive. It would
not be discriminatory to require another equally

*valid form of identification that did not screen
out persons with disabilities.*

*[I]t would be a violation for a store to impose a
rule that no blind or deaf person would be allowed in the store. Further, it would be a violation for such an establishment to invade such individuals' privacy by trying to identify unneces-
sarily the existence of a disability - for example,
by asking whether a person has a disability, by
forcing the person to disclose medical records, or
by requiring the person to undergo an exam or to
determine whether the person has a disability.*

*A public accommodation may, however, impose
neutral rules and criteria that are necessary for
the safe operation of its business. For example, a
height limitation for certain rides in an amusement park may screen out certain persons with
disabilities of short stature, but may still be a legitimate safe criterion. Similarly, it may be a legitimate safety requirement that persons be able
to see in order to operate certain devices or vehicles, even though the effect of this requirement is
to deny access only to those persons with visual
impairments. Safety criteria must, however, be
based on actual risks and not on speculation, stereotypes or generalizations about persons with
disabilities.*

(ii) a failure to make reasonable modifications in
policies, practices, or procedures, when such
modifications are necessary to afford such goods,
services, facilities, privileges, advantages, or accommodations to individuals with disabilities, un-

less the entity can demonstrate that making such modifications would fundamentally alter the nature of such goods, services, facilities, privileges, advantages, or accommodations;

[I]t is discriminatory to refuse to alter a "no pets" rule for a person with a disability who uses a guide or service dog. It would not be a violation of this title to refuse to modify a policy of not touching delicate works of art for a person who is blind if the touching threatened the integrity of the work.

(iii) a failure to take such steps as may be necessary to ensure that no individual with a disability is excluded, denied services, segregated or otherwise treated differently than other individuals because of the absence of auxiliary aids and services, unless the entity can demonstrate that taking such steps would fundamentally alter the nature of the good, service, facility, privilege, advantage, or accommodation being offered or would result in an undue burden;

[A] *store would be required to communicate with a person who is deaf by writing down information which is normally spoken (such as indicating the location of the furniture department). It may be an undue burden, however, for the store to provide an interpreter to convey this information.*

The term "undue burden" is analogous to the term "undue hardship" in title I.

A critical determination is what constitutes an effective auxiliary aid or service (or reasonable accommodation in the employment context). While the use of handwritten notes may be effective to a person who is deaf in the context of shopping, it may not be an effective means of communication in a training session for employees in the employment context. Likewise, while it may not be necessary to provide braille price tags for shoppers who are visually impaired, it may be necessary to provide braille manuals in the employment context. For this reason, the obligations of a business will vary depending on the context involved.

Open-captioning of feature films playing in movie theaters is not required by this Act. Filmmakers are encouraged, however, to produce and distribute open-captioned versions of films and theaters are encouraged to have at least some pre- -announced screenings of captioned versions of feature films.

(iv) a failure to remove architectural barriers, and communication barriers that are structural in nature, in existing facilities, and transportation barriers in existing vehicles and rail passenger cars used by an establishment for transporting individuals (not including barriers that can only be removed through the retrofitting of vehicles or rail passenger cars by the installation of a hydraulic or other lift), where such removal is readily achievable; and

(v) where an entity can demonstrate that the removal of a barrier under clause (iv) is not readily achievable, a failure to make such goods, services, facilities, privileges, advantages, or accommodations available through alternative methods if such methods are readily achievable.

One major obstacle for persons with disabilities is simply obtaining access into buildings. Buildings have often been constructed in such a manner that persons with disabilities are effectively excluded from such places - they cannot get through the door, get around and use the building, or go to another floor.

This title sets out accessibility standards for buildings containing public accommodations. Three situations are covered: existing facilities, alterations, and new construction.

The "readily achievable" and "readily accessible" standards are quite different. Readily achievable is defined as meaning an action which is easily accomplishable without much difficulty or expense.

"Readily accessible to and usable by" is a higher standard, and has been used in a number of previous laws requiring accessibility. It is intended to enable persons with disabilities to get to, enter and use a facility. Although it does not mean total accessibility in every part of every area of a facility, it does mean a high degree of convenient accessibility: for example, accessible routes to and throughout a facility, accessible entrances to

buildings and spaces, usable bathrooms, water fountains and other features.

For example, many banks provide automatic teller machines (ATMs) for use of their customers. A bank with existing ATMs would have to remove barriers associated with the ATM if removal is readily achievable - easily accomplished without much difficulty or expense. Providing a small ramp to avoid a few steps may be readily achievable, but raising or lowering the ATM may be too difficult or expensive. If no readily achievable changes were possible, then the bank would have to provide service through alternative methods.

For new construction and alterations, the purpose is to ensure that the service offered to persons with disabilities is equal to the service offered to others. It would be a violation of this title to build a new bank with ATMs that were not readily accessible to and usable by persons with disabilities. It is not sufficient that the person with a disability can conduct business inside the bank. The ATMs provide an additional service which must be made available to persons with disabilities.

When identical features will generally be used in different ways once the new building is occupied, each one should be accessible in most situations. For example, in a convention center, each of the many identical meeting rooms should be accessible, because they will house meetings on different subjects when the building is in use. Howev-

er, *although each restroom in a new facility must be accessible, it is not necessary that every stall within the bathroom have access features.*

For existing facilities, it is discriminatory to fail to remove structural architectural and communications barriers, if such removal is readily achievable (i.e., easily accomplishable without much difficulty or expense). If it can be demonstrated that removal is not readily achievable, then goods or services must be provided through alternative methods, if such methods are readily achievable.

This readily achievable analysis must be done on a case by case basis. The readily achievable standard provides flexibility for public accommodations to remove barriers and provide access for persons with disabilities.

(B) Fixed Route System.

(i) Accessibility. It shall be considered discrimination for a private entity which operates a fixed route system and which is not subject to section 304 to purchase or lease a vehicle with a seating capacity in excess of 16 passengers (including the driver) for use on such system, for which a solicitation is made after the 30th day following the effective date of this subparagraph, that is not readily accessible to and usable by individuals with disabilities, including individuals who use wheelchairs.

(ii) Equivalent Service. If a private entity which operates a fixed route system and which is not subject to section 304 purchases or leases a vehicle with a seating capacity of 16 passengers or less (including the driver) for use on such system after the effective date of this subparagraph that is not readily accessible to or usable by individuals with disabilities, it shall be considered discrimination for such entity to fail to operate such system so that, when viewed in its entirety, such system ensures a level of service to individuals with disabilities, including individuals who use wheelchairs, equivalent to the level of service provided to individuals without disabilities.

(C) Demand Responsive System. For purposes of subsection (a), discrimination includes

(i) a failure of a private entity which operates a demand responsive system and which is not subject to section 304 to operate such system so that, when viewed in its entirety, such system ensures a level of service to individuals with disabilities, including individuals who use wheelchairs, equivalent to the level of service provided to individuals without disabilities; and

(ii) the purchase or lease by such entity for use on such system of a vehicle with a seating capacity in excess of 16 passengers (including the driver), for which solicitations are made after the 30th day following the effective date of this subparagraph, that is not readily accessible to and usable by individuals with disabilities (including individuals who use wheelchairs) unless such entity can demonstrate that such system, when viewed in its entirety, provides a level of service to individuals with disabilities equivalent to that provided to individuals without disabilities.

(D) Over-The-Road Buses.

(i) Limitation on Applicability. Subparagraphs (B) and (C) do not apply to over-the road buses.

(ii) Accessibility Requirements. For purposes of subsection (a), discrimination includes (I) the purchase or lease of an over-the-road bus which does not comply with the regulations issued under section 306(a)(2) by a private entity which provides transportation of individuals and which is not primarily engaged in the business of transporting people, and (II) any other failure of such entity to comply with such regulations.

(3) Specific Construction. Nothing in this title shall require an entity to permit an individual to participate in or benefit from the goods, services, facilities, privileges, advantages and accommodations of such entity where such individual poses a direct threat to the health or safety of others. The term "direct threat" means a significant risk to the health or safety of others that cannot be eliminated by a modification of policies, practices, or procedures or by the provision of auxiliary aids or services.

Section 303. New Construction and Alterations in Public Accommodations and Commercial Facilities

(a) Application of Term. Except as provided in subsection (b), as applied to public accommodations and commercial facilities, discrimination for purposes of section 302(a) includes

(1) a failure to design and construct facilities for first occupancy later than 30 months after the date of enactment of this Act that are readily accessible to and usable by individuals with disabilities, except where an entity can demonstrate that it is structurally impracticable to meet the requirements of such subsection in accordance with standards set forth or incorporated by reference in regulations issued under this title; and

(2) with respect to a facility or part thereof that is altered by, on behalf of, or for the use of an establishment in a manner that affects or could affect the usability of the facility or part thereof, a failure to make alterations in such a manner that, to the maximum extent feasible, the altered portions of the facility are readily accessible to and usable by individuals with disabilities, including individuals who use wheelchairs. Where the entity is undertaking an alteration that affects or could affect usability of or access to an area of the facility containing a primary function, the entity shall also make the alterations in such a manner that, to the maximum extent feasible, the path of travel to the altered area and the bathrooms, telephones, and drinking fountains serving the altered area, are readily accessible to and usable by individuals with disabilities where such alterations to the path of travel or the bathrooms, telephones, and drinking fountains serving the altered area are not disproportionate to the overall alterations in terms of cost and scope (as determined under criteria established by the Attorney General).

(b) Elevator. Subsection (a) shall not be construed to require the installation of an elevator for facilities that are less than three stories or have less than 3,000 square feet per story unless the building is a shopping center, a shopping mall, or the professional office of a health care provider or unless the Attorney General determines that a particular category of such facilities requires the installation of elevators based on the usage of such facilities.

[T]he requirement of "readily accessible to and usable by" individuals with disabilities contemplates a high degree of convenient accessibility. Essentially, it is designed to ensure that patrons and employees of public accommodations and commercial facilities are able to get to, enter and use the facility.

For potential patrons, this means accessibility of parking areas, accessible routes to, from and into the facility, usable bathrooms and water fountains, and access to the goods, services, and programs of the facility. For example, a new building should be designed so that a potential patron can get to a store, get into the store, and get to the areas where goods are being provided.

For potential employees, the requirement of "readily accessible to and usable by" includes the same types of access, although such individuals require access to and around the employment area, rather than to the area where goods or services are being provided. For example, a new building should be designed so that a potential employee can get to the building, get into the building and get to and around the employment area. It is not required, however, that all individual workstations be constructed in a fully accessible manner, with, for example, accessible features such as lowered shelves and counters.

Such modifications in a particular workstation would be instituted as a "reasonable accommodation" if a particular employee requires such modifications and if they did not constitute an undue hardship.

The rationale for making new construction accessible applies with equal force to alterations. The ADA is geared to the future - the goal being that, over time, access will be the rule rather than the exception. Thus, the bill only requires modest expenditures to provide access in existing facilities, while requiring all new construction to be accessible. The provision governing alterations is akin to new construction because it is only applicable to situations where the commercial facility itself has chosen to alter the premises.

This provision does not require alterations. Rather it simply provides that, when alterations are being made, they must be done in a manner such that, to the maximum extent feasible, the altered area is readily accessible to and usable by individuals with disabilities. It simply makes no sense to alter premises in a manner that does not consider access.

A public accommodation or commercial facility may not evade the path of travel, accessible restrooms, and other requirements by performing a series of small alterations which it would otherwise have performed as a single undertaking. For example, if a public accommodation has completed an alteration without incorporating an accessible path of travel, accessible restrooms, and other requirements, the total costs of the prior alterations plus others that are or will be proximate in time may be considered in determining whether providing an accessible path of trav-

el, restrooms, telephones and bathrooms is disproportionate.

If the aggregate cost of an accessible path of travel, accessible restrooms, telephones, and drinking fountains would be disproportionate to the overall alteration cost, the public accommodation is not relieved of the obligation to provide a number of such features that are not disproportionate. The goal is to provide a maximum degree of accessibility in such features without exceeding the disproportionality limit.

If a selection must be made between accessibility features, those which provide the greatest use of the facility [should] be selected. For example, an accessible entrance would generally be the most important path of travel features, since without it the facility will be totally unusable by many persons with disabilities. An accessible restroom would have greater priority than an accessible drinking fountain.

If there is no way to provide an accessible path of travel to an altered area because of the disproportionality limit, making restrooms, telephones and drinking fountains serving the area accessible is still required if it is not disproportionate. Some individuals with disabilities can negotiate steps but still need accessibility features in restrooms, drinking fountains, and telephones.

Section 304. Prohibition of Discrimination in Specified Public Transportation Services Provided by Private Entities

(a) General Rule. No individual shall be discriminated against on the basis of disability in the full and equal enjoyment of specified public transportation services provided by a private entity that is primarily engaged in the business of transporting people and whose operations affect commerce.

(b) Construction. For purposes of subsection (a), discrimination includes

(1) the imposition or application by an entity described in subsection (a) of eligibility criteria that screen out or tend to screen out an individual with a disability or any class of individuals with disabilities from fully enjoying the specified public transportation services provided by the entity, unless such criteria can be shown to be necessary for the provision of the services being offered;

(2) the failure of such entity to

(A) make reasonable modifications consistent with those required under section 302(b)(2)(A)(ii);

(B) provide auxiliary aids and services consistent with the requirements of section 302(b)(2)(A)(iii); and

(C) remove barriers consistent with the requirements of section 302(b)(2)(A) and with the requirements of section 303(a)(2);

(3) the purchase or lease by such entity of a new vehicle (other than an automobile, a van with a seating capacity of less than 8 passengers, including the driver, or an over-the-road bus) which is to be used to provide specified public transportation and for which a solicita-

tion is made after the 30th day following the effective
date of this section, that is not readily accessible to and
usable by individuals with disabilities, including individuals who use wheelchairs; except that the new vehicle need not be readily accessible to and usable by such
individuals if the new vehicle is to be used solely in a
demand responsive system and if the entity can demonstrate that such system, when viewed in its entirety,
provides a level of service to such individuals equivalent to the level of service provided to the general public;

(4)(A) the purchase or lease by such entity of an over-
the-road bus which does not comply with the regulations issued under section 306(a)(2); and

(B) any other failure of such entity to comply with
such regulations; and

(5) the purchase or lease by such entity of a new van
with a seating capacity of less than 8 passengers, including the driver, which is to be used to provide specified public transportation and for which a solicitation
is made after the 30th day following the effective date
of this section that is not readily accessible to or usable
by individuals with disabilities, including individuals
who use wheelchairs; except that the new van need not
be readily accessible to and usable by such individuals
if the entity can demonstrate that the system for which
the van is being purchased or leased, when viewed in
its entirety, provides a level of service to such individuals equivalent to the level of service provided to the
general public;

(6) the purchase or lease by such entity of a new rail passenger car that is to be used to provide specified public transportation, and for which a solicitation is made later than 30 days after the effective date of this paragraph, that is not readily accessible to and usable by individuals with disabilities, including individuals who use wheelchairs; and

(7) the remanufacture by such entity of a rail passenger car that is to be used to provide specified public transportation so as to extend its usable life for 10 years or more, or the purchase or lease by such entity of such a rail car, unless the rail car, to the maximum extent feasible, is made readily accessible to and usable by individuals with disabilities, including individuals who use wheelchairs.

(c) Historical or Antiquated Cars.

(1) Exception. To the extent that compliance with subsection (b)(2)(C) or (b)(7) would significantly alter the historic or antiquated character of a historical or antiquated rail passenger car, or a rail station served exclusively by such cars, or would result in violation of any rule, regulation, standard, or order issued by the Secretary of Transportation under the Federal Railroad Safety Act of 1970, such compliance shall not be required.

(2) Definition. As used in this subsection, the term "historical or antiquated rail passenger car" means a rail passenger car

(A) which is not less than 30 years old at the time of its use for transporting individuals;

(B) the manufacturer of which is no longer in the business of manufacturing rail passenger cars; and

(C) which

(i) has a consequential association with events or persons significant to the past; or

(ii) embodies, or is being restored to embody, the distinctive characteristics of a type of rail passenger car used in the past, or to represent a time period which has passed.

Section 305. Study

(a) Purposes. The Office of Technology Assessment shall undertake a study to determine

(1) the access needs of individuals with disabilities to over-the-road buses and over-the-road bus service; and

(2) the most cost-effective methods for providing access to over-the-road buses and over-the-road bus service to individuals with disabilities, particularly individuals who use wheelchairs, through all forms of boarding options.

(b) Contents. The study shall include, at a minimum, an analysis of the following:

(1) The anticipated demand by individuals with disabilities for accessible over-the-road buses and over-the-road bus service.

(2) The degree to which such buses and service, including any service required under sections 304(b)(4) and 306(a)(2), are readily accessible to and usable by individuals with disabilities.

(3) The effectiveness of various methods of providing accessibility to such buses and service to individuals with disabilities.

(4) The cost of providing accessible over-the-road buses and bus service to individuals with disabilities, including consideration of recent technological and cost saving developments in equipment and devices.

(5) Possible design changes in over-the-road buses that could enhance accessibility, including the installation of accessible restrooms which do not result in a loss of seating capacity.

(6) The impact of accessibility requirements on the continuation of over-the-road bus service, with particular consideration of the impact of such requirements on such service to rural communities.

(c) Advisory committee. In conducting the study required by subsection (a), the Office of Technology Assessment shall establish an advisory committee, which shall consist of

(1) members selected from among private operators and manufacturers of over-the-road buses;

(2) members selected from among individuals with disabilities, particularly individuals who use wheelchairs, who are potential riders of such buses; and

(3) members selected for their technical expertise on issues included in the study, including manufacturers of boarding assistance equipment and devices.

The number of members selected under each of paragraphs (1) and (2) shall be equal, and the total number of members selected under paragraphs (1) and (2) shall exceed the number of members selected under paragraph (3).

(d) Deadline. The study required by subsection (a), along with recommendations by the Office of Technology Assessment, including any policy options for legislative action, shall be submitted to the President and Congress within 36 months after the date of the enactment of this Act. If the President determines that compliance with the regulations issued pursuant to section 306(a)(2)(B) on or before the applicable deadlines specified in section 306(a)(2)(B) will result in a significant reduction in intercity over-the-road bus service, the President shall extend each such deadline by 1 year.

(e) Review. In developing the study required by subsection (a), the Office of Technology Assessment shall provide a preliminary draft of such study to the Architectural and Transportation Barriers Compliance Board established under section 502 of the Rehabilitation Act of 1973. The Board shall have an opportunity to comment on such draft study, and any such comments by the Board made in writing within 120 days after the Board's receipt of the draft study shall be incorporated as part of the final study required to be submitted under subsection (d).

Section 306. Regulations

(a) Transportation Provisions.

(1) General Rule. Not later than 1 year after the date of the enactment of this Act, the Secretary of Transportation shall issue regulations in an accessible format to carry out sections 302(b)(2)(B) and (C) and to carry out section 304 (other than subsection (b)(4)).

(2) Special Rules for Providing Access to Over-the-Road Buses.

(A) Interim Requirements.

(i) Issuance. Not later than 1 year after the date of the enactment of this Act, the Secretary of Transportation shall issue regulations in an accessible format to carry out sections 304(b)(4) and 302(b)(2)(D)(ii) that require each private entity which uses an over-the-road bus to provide transportation of individuals to provide accessibility to such bus; except that such regulations shall not require any structural changes in over-the-road buses in order to provide access to individuals who use wheelchairs during the effective period of such regulations and shall not require the purchase of boarding assistance devices to provide access to such individuals.

(ii) Effective Period. The regulations issued pursuant to this subparagraph shall be effective until the effective date of the regulations issued under subparagraph (B).

(B) Final Requirement.

(i) Review of Study and Interim Requirements. The Secretary shall review the study submitted under section 305 and the regulations issued pursuant to subparagraph (A).

(ii) Issuance. Not later than 1 year after the date of the submission of the study under section 305, the Secretary shall issue in an accessible format new regulations to carry out sections 304(b)(4) and 302(b)(2)(D)(ii) that require, taking into account the purposes of the study under section 305 and any recommendations resulting from such study, each private entity which uses an over-the-road bus to provide transportation to individuals to provide accessibility to such bus to individuals with disabilities, including individuals who use wheelchairs.

(iii) Effective Period. Subject to section 305(d), the regulations issued pursuant to this subparagraph shall take effect

(I) with respect to small providers of transportation (as defined by the Secretary), 7 years after the date of the enactment of this Act; and

(II) with respect to other providers of transportation, 6 years after such date of enactment.

(C) Limitation on Requiring Installation of Accessible Restrooms. The regulations issued pursuant to this paragraph shall not require the installation of accessible restrooms in over-the-road buses if such installation would result in a loss of seating capacity.

(3) Standards. The regulations issued pursuant to this subsection shall include standards applicable to facilities and vehicles covered by sections 302(b)(2) and 304.

(b) Other Provisions. Not later than 1 year after the date of the enactment of this Act, the Attorney General shall issue regulations in an accessible format to carry out the provisions of this title not referred to in subsection (a) that include standards applicable to facilities and vehicles covered under section 302.

(c) Consistency with ATBCB Guidelines. Standards included in regulations issued under subsections (a) and (b) shall be consistent with the minimum guidelines and requirements issued by the Architectural and Transportation Barriers Compliance Board in accordance with section 504 of this Act.

(d) Interim Accessibility Standards.

(1) Facilities. If final regulations have not been issued pursuant to this section, for new construction or alterations for which a valid and appropriate State or local building permit is obtained prior to the issuance of final regulations under this section, and for which the construction or alteration authorized by such permit begins within one year of the receipt of such permit and is

completed under the terms of such permit, compliance with the Uniform Federal Accessibility Standards in effect at the time the building permit is issued shall suffice to satisfy the requirement that facilities be readily accessible to and usable by persons with disabilities as required under section 303, except that, if such final regulations have not been issued one year after the Architectural and Transportation Barriers Compliance Board has issued the supplemental minimum guidelines required under section 504(a) of this Act, compliance with such supplemental minimum guidelines shall be necessary to satisfy the requirement that facilities be readily accessible to and usable by persons with disabilities prior to issuance of the final regulations.

(2) Vehicles and Rail Passenger Cars. If final regulations have not been issued pursuant to this section, a private entity shall be considered to have complied with the requirements of this title, if any, that a vehicle or rail passenger car be readily accessible to and usable by individuals with disabilities, if the design for such vehicle or car complies with the laws and regulations (including the Minimum Guidelines and Requirements for Accessible Design and such supplemental minimum guidelines as are issued under section 504(a) of this Act) governing accessibility of such vehicles or cars, to the extent that such laws and regulations are not inconsistent with this title and are in effect at the time such design is substantially completed.

Section 307. Exemptions for Private Clubs and Religious Organizations

The provisions of this title shall not apply to private clubs or establishments exempted from coverage under title II of the Civil Rights Act of 1964 or to religious organizations or entities controlled by religious organizations, including places of worship.

The exemption for private clubs is intended to operate in the same narrow manner as in title II of the Civil Rights Act of 1964.

The Committee does not intend to cover under this title religious organizations or entities controlled by religious organizations, including places of worship. Thus a church sanctuary would not be required to make its facilities accessible to and usable by disabled persons, nor to construct new facilities in such a manner.

In order to qualify for this exemption, the entity must be controlled by a religious organization, as that concept has been applied in other civil rights laws, such as in the exemption provided under title IX of the Education Amendments of 1972, as amended by the Civil Rights Restoration Act.

Section 308. Enforcement

(a) In General.

(1) Availability of Remedies and Procedures. The remedies and procedures set forth in section 204(a) of the Civil Rights Act of 1964 are the remedies and procedures this title provides to any person who is be-

ing subjected to discrimination on the basis of disability in violation of this title or who has reasonable grounds for believing that such person is about to be subjected to discrimination in violation of section 303. Nothing in this section shall require a person with a disability to engage in a futile gesture if such person has actual notice that a person or organization covered by this title does not intend to comply with its provisions.

(2) Injunctive Relief. In the case of violations of section 302(b)(2)(A)(iv) and section 303(a), injunctive relief shall include an order to alter facilities to make such facilities readily accessible to and usable by individuals with disabilities to the extent required by this title. Where appropriate, injunctive relief shall also include requiring the provision of an auxiliary aid or service, modification of a policy, or provision of alternative methods, to the extent required by this title.

(b) Enforcement by the Attorney General.

(1) Denial of Rights.

(A) Duty to Investigate.

(i) In General. The Attorney General shall investigate alleged violations of this title, and shall undertake periodic reviews of compliance of covered entities under this title.

(ii) Attorney General Certification. On the application of a State or local government, the Attorney General may, in consultation with the Architectural and Transportation Barriers Compliance

Board, and after prior notice and a public hearing at which persons, including individuals with disabilities, are provided an opportunity to testify against such certification, certify that a State law or local building code or similar ordinance that establishes accessibility requirements meets or exceeds the minimum requirements of this Act for the accessibility and usability of covered facilities under this title. At any enforcement proceeding under this section, such certification by the Attorney General shall be rebuttable evidence that such State law or local ordinance does meet or exceed the minimum requirements of this Act.

(B) Potential Violation. If the Attorney General has reasonable cause to believe that

(i) any person or group of persons is engaged in a pattern or practice of discrimination under this title; or

(ii) any person or group of persons has been discriminated against under this title and such discrimination raises an issue of general public importance,

the Attorney General may commence a civil action in any appropriate United States district court.

(2) Authority of Court. In a civil action under paragraph (1)(B), the court

(A) may grant any equitable relief that such court considers to be appropriate, including, to the extent required by this title

(i) granting temporary, preliminary, or permanent relief;

(ii) providing an auxiliary aid or service, modification of policy, practice, or procedure, or alternative method; and

(iii) making facilities readily accessible to and usable by individuals with disabilities;

(B) may award such other relief as the court considers to be appropriate, including monetary damages to persons aggrieved when requested by the Attorney General; and

(C) may, to vindicate the public interest, assess a civil penalty against the entity in an amount

(i) not exceeding $50,000 for a first violation; and

(ii) not exceeding $100,000 for any subsequent violation.

(3) Single Violation. For purposes of paragraph (2)(C), in determining whether a first or subsequent violation has occurred, a determination in a single action, by judgment or settlement, that the covered entity has engaged in more than one discriminatory act shall be counted as a single violation.

(4) Punitive Damages. For purposes of subsection (b)(2)(B), the term "monetary damages" and "such other relief" does not include punitive damages.

(5) Judicial Consideration. In a civil action under paragraph (1)(B), the court, when considering what amount
of civil penalty, if any, is appropriate, shall give consideration to any good faith effort or attempt to comply
with this Act by the entity. In evaluating good faith,
the court shall consider, among other factors it deems
relevant, whether the entity could have reasonably anticipated the need for an appropriate type of auxiliary
aid needed to accommodate the unique needs of a particular individual with a disability.

*[I]f the remedies and procedures change in title II of the
1964 Civil Rights Act, for persons discriminated against
in public accommodations on account of race, color, religion, or national origin, they will change identically in
this title for persons with disabilities.*

*The Attorney General has a three part obligation: (1) to
investigate alleged violations of title III and to conduct
periodic reviews of compliance, (2) to certify that state
laws or local building codes meet or exceed requirements
of the bill and (3) to bring cases that indicate a pattern or
practice of discrimination or that are of general public
importance.*

*The Attorney General is required to investigate alleged vi-
olations of this title, and to conduct periodic reviews to
evaluate whether covered entities are complying with this
title. This duty of the Attorney General is essential to effective enforcement of this title.*

Section 309. Examinations and Courses

Any person that offers examinations or courses related to
applications, licensing, certification, or credentialing for

secondary or post-secondary education, professional, or trade purposes shall offer such examinations or courses in a place and manner accessible to persons with disabilities or offer alternative accessible arrangements for such individuals.

[S]tates often require the licenses provided by such authorities in order for an individual to practice a particular profession or trade. Thus, this provision was adopted in order to assure that persons with disabilities are not foreclosed from educational, professional or trade opportunities because an examination or course is conducted in an inaccessible site or without an accommodation.

Under this requirement an entity cannot offer its program in an inaccessible site without providing persons with disabilities an alternative accessible arrangement which provides comparable conditions to those provided to others. For example, the entity could not give a course or a test in an accessible classroom and then offer the person with the disability the test in a cold, poorly lit basement.

Section 310. Effective Date

(a) General Rule. Except as provided in subsections (b) and (c), this title shall become effective 18 months after the date of the enactment of this Act.

(b) Civil Actions. Except for any civil action brought for a violation of section 303, no civil action shall be brought for any act or omission described in section 302 which occurs

(1) during the first 6 months after the effective date, against businesses that employ 25 or fewer employees and have gross receipts of $1,000,000 or less; and

(2) during the first year after the effective date, against businesses that employ 10 or fewer employees and have gross receipts of $500,000 or less.

(c) Exception. Sections 302(a) for purposes of section 302(b)(2)(B) and (C) only, 304(a) for purposes of section 304(b)(3) only, 304(b)(3), 305, and 306 shall take effect on the date of the enactment of this Act.

Title IV - Telecommunications

TITLE IV - TELECOMMUNICATIONS

This title amends the Communications Act of 1934, to make telecommunications services available to hearing and speech impaired persons. This title requires a national relay service to be established so persons with disabilities can communicate with other persons using telecommunications devices.

Section 401. Telecommunications Relay Services for Hearing-Impaired and Speech-Impaired Individuals

(a) Telecommunications. Title II of the Communications Act of 1934 is amended by adding at the end thereof the following new section:

"Section 225. Telecommunications Services for Hearing-Impaired and Speech-Impaired Individuals

"(a) Definitions. As used in this section

"(1) Common Carrier or Carrier. The term 'common carrier' or 'carrier' includes any common carrier engaged in interstate communication by wire or radio as defined in section 3(h) and any common carrier engaged in intrastate communication by wire or radio, notwithstanding sections 2(b) and 221(b).

"(2) TDD. The term 'TDD' means a Telecommunications Device for the Deaf, which is a machine that employs graphic communication in the transmission of coded signals through a wire or radio communication system.

"(3) Telecommunications Relay Services. 'The term 'telecommunications relay services' means telephone transmission services that provide the ability for an individual who has a hearing impairment or speech impairment to engage in communication by wire or radio with a hearing individual in a manner that is functionally equivalent to the ability of an individual who does not have a hearing impairment or speech impairment to communicate using voice communication services by wire or radio. Such term includes services that enable two-way communication between an individual who uses a TDD or other nonvoice terminal device and an individual who does not use such a device.

"(b) Availability of Telecommunications Relay Services.

"(1) In General. In order to carry out the purposes established under section 1, to make available to all individuals in the United States a rapid, efficient nationwide communication service, and to increase the utility of the telephone system of the Nation, the [Federal Communications] Commission shall ensure that interstate and intrastate telecommunications relay services are available, to the extent possible and in the most efficient manner, to hearing-impaired and speech-impaired individuals in the United States.

"(2) Use of General Authority and Remedies. For the purposes of administering and enforcing the provisions of this section and the regulations prescribed thereunder, the Commission shall have

the same authority, power, and functions with respect to common carriers engaged in intrastate
communication as the Commission has in administering and enforcing the provisions of this title
with respect to any common carrier engaged in
interstate communication. Any violation of this
section by any common carrier engaged in intrastate communication shall be subject to the same
remedies, penalties, and procedures as are applicable to a violation of this Act by a common carrier
engaged in interstate communication.

"(c) Provision of Services. Each common carrier providing telephone voice transmission services shall,
not later than 3 years after the date of enactment of
this section, provide in compliance with the regulations prescribed under this section, throughout the
area in which it offers service, telecommunications
relay services, individually, through designees,
through a competitively selected vendor, or in concert with other carriers. A common carrier shall be
considered to be in compliance with such regulations.

"(1) with respect to intrastate telecommunications
relay services in any State that does not have a
certified program under subsection (f) and with
respect to interstate telecommunications relay
services, if such common carrier (or other entity
through which the carrier is providing such relay
services) is in compliance with the Commission's
regulations under subsection (d); or

"(2) with respect to intrastate telecommunications
relay services in any State that has a certified

program under subsection (f) for such State, if such common carrier (or other entity through which the carrier is providing such relay services) is in compliance with the program certified under subsection (f) for such State.

"(d) Regulations.

"(1) In General. The Commission shall, not later than 1 year after the date of enactment of this section, prescribe regulations to implement this section, including regulations that

"(A) establish functional requirements, guidelines, and operations procedures for telecommunications relay services;

"(B) establish minimum standards that shall be met in carrying out subsection (c);

"(C) require that telecommunications relay services operate every day for 24 hours per day;

"(D) require that users of telecommunications relay services pay rates no greater than the rates paid for functionally equivalent voice communication services with respect to such factors as the duration of the call, the time of day, and the distance from point of origination to point of termination;

"(E) prohibit relay operators from failing to fulfill the obligations of common carriers by refusing calls or limiting the length of calls that use telecommunications relay services;

"(F) prohibit relay operators from disclosing the content of any relayed conversation and from keeping records of the content of any such conversation beyond the duration of the call; and

"(G) prohibit relay operators from intentionally altering a relayed conversation.

"(2) Technology. The Commission shall ensure that regulations prescribed to implement this section encourage, consistent with section 7(a) of this Act, the use of existing technology and do not discourage or impair the development of improved technology.

"(3) Jurisdictional Separation of Costs.

"(A) In General. Consistent with the provisions of section 410 of this Act, the Commission shall prescribe regulations governing the jurisdictional separation of costs for the services provided pursuant to this section.

"(B) Recovering Costs. Such regulations shall generally provide that costs caused by interstate telecommunications relay services shall be recovered from all subscribers for every interstate service and costs caused by intrastate telecommunications relay services shall be recovered from the intrastate jurisdiction. In a State that has a certified program under subsection (f), a State commission shall permit a common carrier to recover the costs incurred in providing intrastate telecommunications relay services by a method consistent with the requirements of this section.

"(e) Enforcement.

"(1) In General. Subject to subsections (f) and (g), the Commission shall enforce this section.

"(2) Complaint. The Commission shall resolve, by final order, a complaint alleging a violation of this section within 180 days after the date such complaint is filed.

"(f) Certification.

"(1) State Documentation. Any State desiring to establish a State program under this section shall submit documentation to the Commission that describes the program of such State for implementing intrastate telecommunications relay services and the procedures and remedies available for enforcing any requirements imposed by the State program.

"(2) Requirements for Certification. After review of such documentation, the Commission shall certify the State program if the Commission determines that

"(A) the program makes available to hearing-impaired and speech-impaired individuals, either directly, through designees, through a competitively selected vendor, or through regulation of intrastate common carriers, intrastate telecommunications relay services in such State in a manner that meets or exceeds the requirements of regulations prescribed by the Commission under subsection (d); and

"(B) the program makes available adequate procedures and remedies for enforcing the requirements of the State program.

"(3) Method of Funding. Except as provided in subsection (d), the Commission shall not refuse to certify a State program based solely on the method such State will implement for funding intrastate telecommunication relay services.

"(4) Suspension or Revocation of Certification. The Commission may suspend or revoke such certification if, after notice and opportunity for hearing, the Commission determines that such certification is no longer warranted. In a State whose program has been suspended or revoked, the Commission shall take such steps as may be necessary, consistent with this section, to ensure continuity of telecommunications relay services.

"(g) Complaint.

"(1) Referral of Complaint. If a complaint to the Commission alleges a violation of this section with respect to intrastate telecommunications relay services within a State and certification of the program of such State under subsection (f) is in effect, the Commission shall refer such complaint to such State.

"(2) Jurisdiction of Commission. After referring a complaint to a State under paragraph (1), the Commission shall exercise jurisdiction over such complaint only if

"(A) final action under such State program has not been taken on such complaint by such State

"(i) within 180 days after the complaint is filed with such State; or

"(ii) within a shorter period as prescribed by the regulations of such State; or

"(B) the Commission determines that such State program is no longer qualified for certification under subsection (f).".

(b) Conforming Amendments. The Communications Act of 1934 is amended

(1) in section 2(b), by striking "section 224" and inserting "sections 224 and 225"; and

(2) in section 221(b), by striking "section 301" and inserting "sections 225 and 301".

Section 402. Closed-Captioning of Public Service Announcements

Section 711 of the Communications Act of 1934 is amended to read as follows:

"Section 711. Closed-Captioning of Public Service Announcements

"Any television public service announcement that is produced or funded in whole or in part by any agency or instrumentality of Federal Government shall include closed captioning of the verbal content of such announcement. A television broadcast station licensee

"(1) shall not be required to supply closed captioning for any such announcement that fails to include it; and

"(2) shall not be liable for broadcasting any such announcement without transmitting a closed caption unless the licensee intentionally fails to transmit the closed caption that was included with the announcement.".

Title V
Miscellaneous Provisions

TITLE V - MISCELLANEOUS PROVISIONS

Section 501. Construction

(a) In General. Except as otherwise provided in this Act, nothing in this Act shall be construed to apply a lesser standard than the standards applied under title V of the Rehabilitation Act of 1973 or the regulations issued by Federal agencies pursuant to such title.

(b) Relationship to Other Laws. Nothing in this Act shall be construed to invalidate or limit the remedies, rights, and procedures of any Federal law or law of any State or political subdivision of any State or jurisdiction that provides greater or equal protection for the rights of individuals with disabilities than are afforded by this Act. Nothing in this Act shall be construed to preclude the prohibition of, or the imposition of restrictions on, smoking in places of employment covered by title I, in transportation covered by title II or III, or in places of public accommodation covered by title III.

(c) Insurance. Titles I through IV of this Act shall not be construed to prohibit or restrict

(1) an insurer, hospital or medical service company, health maintenance organization, or any agent, or entity that administers benefit plans, or similar organizations from underwriting risks, classifying risks, or administering such risks that are based on or not inconsistent with State law; or

(2) a person or organization covered by this Act from establishing, sponsoring, observing or administering the terms of a bona fide benefit plan that are based on underwriting risks, classifying risks, or administering such

risks that are based on or not inconsistent with State law; or

(3) a person or organization covered by this Act from establishing, sponsoring, observing or administering the terms of a bona fide benefit plan that is not subject to State laws that regulate insurance.

Paragraphs (1), (2), and (3) shall not be used as a subterfuge to evade the purposes of title I and III.

(d) Accommodations and Services. Nothing in this Act shall be construed to require an individual with a disability to accept an accommodation, aid, service, opportunity, or benefit which such individual chooses not to accept.

This section describes the relationship between the ADA and the Rehabilitation Act of 1973 and other laws. This section also describes the relationship between the ADA and insurance. Finally, the section provides an individual with a disability the right to decline a separate service or accommodation.

A plaintiff may choose to pursue claims under a state law that does not confer greater substantive rights, or even confers fewer substantive rights, if the plaintiff's situation is protected under the alternative law and the remedies are greater. For example, the California Fair Enforcement and Housing Act (FEHA) does not cover persons with mental disabilities. However, the FEHA has been construed to provide compensatory and punitive damages. Because the ADA covers mental disabilities, the FEHA could be construed as not conferring equal or greater rights than the ADA. However, a person with a physical disability may choose to sue under the FEHA, as well as under the ADA, because of the availability of damages under the FEHA. Section 501(b) ensures that the FEHA is not preempted by the ADA.

Section 501(c) may not, however, be used as a subterfuge to evade the requirements of this Act pertaining to employment, public services, and public accommodations regardless of the date an insurance or employer benefit plan was adopted.

For example, an employer could not deny a qualified applicant a job because the employer's current insurance plan does not cover the person's disability or because of an anticipated increase in the costs of the insurance. Moreover, while a plan which limits certain kinds of coverage based on classification of risk would be allowed under this section, the plan may not refuse to insure or refuse to continue to insure, or limit the amount, extent, or kind of coverage available to an individual, or charge a different rate for the same coverage available to an individual, or charge a different rate for the same coverage solely because of a physical or mental impairment, except where the refusal, limitation, or rate differential is based on sound actuarial principles, or is related to actual or reasonably anticipated experience.

For example, a blind person may not be denied coverage on blindness independent of actuarial classification. Likewise, with respect to group health insurance coverage, an individual with a pre-existing condition may be denied coverage for that condition for the period specified in the policy but cannot be denied coverage for illness or injuries unrelated to the non-existing condition. And as noted above, while it is permissible for an employer to offer insurance policies that limit coverage for certain proce-

dures or treatments, coverage cannot be denied entirely to
a person with a disability.

In sum, ADA requires that underwriting and classification
of risks be based on sound actuarial principles or be related to actual or reasonably anticipated experience.

[A] blind individual may choose not to avail himself or
herself of the right to go to the front of a line, even if a
particular public accommodation has chosen to offer such
a modification of a policy for blind individuals. Or, a
blind individual may choose to decline to participate in a
special museum tour that allows persons to touch sculp-
tures in an exhibit and instead tour the exhibits at his or
her own pace with the museum's recorded tour.

Section 502. State Immunity

A State shall not be immune under the eleventh amendment to the Constitution of the United States from an action in Federal or State court of competent jurisdiction
for a violation of this Act. In any action against a State
for a violation of the requirements of this Act, remedies
(including remedies both at law and in equity) are available for such a violation to the same extent as such remedies are available for such a violation in an action against
any public or private entity other than a State.

This section removes immunity of states granted by the
Eleventh Amendment of the Constitution. The Committee intends for states to be covered by the ADA, where
applicable, and to be subject to suit in federal or state
courts. The remedies available against state defendants
are the same as those available against other defendants.

Section 503. Prohibition Against Retaliation and Coercion

(a) Retaliation. No person shall discriminate against any individual because such individual has opposed any act or practice made unlawful by this Act or because such individual made a charge, testified, assisted, or participated in any manner in an investigation, proceeding, or hearing under this Act.

(b) Interference, Coercion, or Intimidation. It shall be unlawful to coerce, intimidate, threaten, or interfere with any individual in the exercise or enjoyment of, or on account of his or her having exercised or enjoyed, or on account of his or her having aided or encouraged any other individual in the exercise or enjoyment of, any right granted or protected by this Act.

(c) Remedies and Procedures. The remedies and procedures available under sections 107, 203, and 308 of this Act shall be available to aggrieved persons for violations of subsections (a) and (b), with respect to title I, title II and title III, respectively.

[A]n individual who was retaliated against in an employment discrimination complaint would have the same remedies and procedures available under Section 107 as an individual alleging employment discrimination.

Section 504. Regulations by the Architectural and Transportation Barriers Compliance Board

(a) Issuance of Guidelines. Not later than 9 months after the date of enactment of this Act, the Architectural and

Transportation Barriers Compliance Board shall issue minimum guidelines that shall supplement the existing Minimum Guidelines and Requirements for Accessible Design for purposes of titles II and III of this Act.

(b) Contents of Guidelines. The supplemental guidelines issued under subsection (a) shall establish additional requirements, consistent with this Act, to ensure that buildings, facilities, rail passenger cars, and vehicles are accessible, in terms of architecture and design, transportation, and communication, to individuals with disabilities.

(c) Qualified Historic Properties.

(1) In General. The supplemental guidelines issued under subsection (a) shall include procedures and requirements for alterations that will threaten or destroy the historic significance of qualified historic buildings and facilities as defined in 4.1.7(1)(a) of the Uniform Federal Accessibility Standards.

(2) Sites Eligible for Listing in National Register. With respect to alterations of buildings or facilities that are eligible for listing in the National Register of Historic Places under the National Historic Preservation Act, the guidelines described in paragraph (1) shall, at a minimum, maintain the procedures and requirements established in 4.1.7(1) and (2) of the Uniform Federal Accessibility Standards.

(3) Other Sites. With respect to alterations of buildings or facilities designated as historic under State or local law, the guidelines described in paragraph (1) shall establish procedures equivalent to those established by 4.1.7(1)(b) and (c) of the Uniform Federal Accessibili-

ty Standards, and shall require, at a minimum, compliance with the requirements established in 4.1.7(2) of such standards.

Section 505. Attorney's Fees

In any action or administrative proceeding commenced pursuant to this Act, the court or agency, in its discretion, may allow the prevailing party, other than the United States, a reasonable attorney's fee, including litigation expenses, and costs, and the United States shall be liable for the foregoing the same as a private individual.

The House Committee on the Judiciary intends that the attorney's fee provision be interpreted in a manner consistent with the Civil Rights Attorney's Fees Act, including that statute's definition of prevailing party, as construed by the Supreme Court.

Litigation expenses include the costs of expert witnesses. This provision explicitly incorporates the phrase "including litigation expenses" to respond to rulings from the Supreme Court that items such as expert witness fees, travel expenses, etc., be explicitly included if intended to be covered under an attorney's fee provision.

Section 506. Technical Assistance

(a) Plan for Assistance.

(1) In General. Not later than 180 days after the date of enactment of this Act, the Attorney General, in consultation with the Chair of the Equal Employment Opportunity Commission, the Secretary of Transportation, the Chair of the Architectural and Transportation Bar-

riers Compliance Board, and the Chairman of the Federal Communications Commission, shall develop a plan to assist entities covered under this Act, and other Federal agencies, in understanding the responsibility of such entities and agencies under this Act.

(2) Publication of Plan. The Attorney General shall publish the plan referred to in paragraph (1) for public comment in accordance with subchapter II of chapter 5 of title 5, United States Code (commonly known as the Administrative Procedure Act).

(b) Agency and Public Assistance. The Attorney General may obtain the assistance of other Federal agencies in carrying out subsection (a), including the National Council on Disability, the President's Committee on Employment of People with Disabilities, the Small Business Administration, and the Department of Commerce.

(c) Implementation.

(1) Rendering Assistance. Each Federal agency that has responsibility under paragraph (2) for implementing this Act may render technical assistance to individuals and institutions that have rights or duties under the respective title or titles for which such agency has responsibility.

(2) Implementation of Titles.

(A) Title I. The Equal Employment Opportunity Commission and the Attorney General shall implement the plan for assistance developed under subsection (a), for title I.

(B) Title II.

(i) Subtitle A. The Attorney General shall implement such plan for assistance for subtitle A of title II.

(ii) Subtitle B. The Secretary of Transportation shall implement such plan for assistance for subtitle B of title II.

(C) Title III. The Attorney General, in coordination with the Secretary of Transportation and the Chair of the Architectural Transportation Barriers Compliance Board, shall implement such plan for assistance for title III, except for section 304, the plan for assistance for which shall be implemented by the Secretary of Transportation.

(D) Title IV. The Chairman of the Federal Communications Commission, in coordination with the Attorney General, shall implement such plan for assistance for title IV.

(3) Technical assistance manuals. Each Federal agency that has responsibility under paragraph (2) for implementing this Act shall, as part of its implementation responsibilities, ensure the availability and provision of appropriate technical assistance manuals to individuals or entities with rights or duties under this Act no later than six months after applicable final regulations are published under titles I, II, III, and IV.

(d) Grants and Contracts.

(1) In General. Each Federal agency that has responsibility under subsection (c)(2) for implementing this Act may make grants or award contracts to effectuate the purposes of this section, subject to the availability of appropriations. Such grants and contracts may be awarded to individuals, institutions not organized for profit and no part of the net earnings of which inures to the benefit of any private shareholder or individual (including educational institutions), and associations representing individuals who have rights or duties under this Act. Contracts may be awarded to entities organized for profit, but such entities may not be the recipients of grants described in this paragraph.

(2) Dissemination of Information. Such grants and contracts, among other uses, may be designed to ensure wide dissemination of information about the rights and duties established by this Act and to provide information and technical assistance about techniques for effective compliance with this Act.

(e) Failure to Receive Assistance. An employer, public accommodation, or other entity covered under this Act shall not be excused from compliance with the requirements of this Act because of any failure to receive technical assistance under this section, including any failure in the development or dissemination of any technical assistance manual authorized by this section.

Section 507. Federal Wilderness Areas

(a) Study. The National Council on Disability shall conduct a study and report on the effect that wilderness designations and wilderness land management practices have on the ability of individuals with disabilities to use and enjoy the National Wilderness Preservation System as established under the Wilderness Act.

(b) Submission of Report. Not later than 1 year after the enactment of this Act, the National Council on Disability shall submit the report required under subsection (a) to Congress.

(c) Specific Wilderness Access.

(1) In General. Congress reaffirms that nothing in the Wilderness Act is to be construed as prohibiting the use of a wheelchair in a wilderness area by an individual whose disability requires use of a wheelchair, and consistent with the Wilderness Act no agency is required to provide any form of special treatment or accommodation, or to construct any facilities or modify any conditions of lands within a wilderness area in order to facilitate such use.

(2) Definition. For purposes of paragraph (1), the term "wheelchair" means a device designed solely for use by a mobility-impaired person for locomotion, that is suitable for use in an indoor pedestrian area.

Under current National Park Service regulations, wheelchairs (both manual and motorized) are allowed access onto park lands, including both designated public parks and protected wilderness areas. Wheelchair users are considered by the Park Service to be pedestrians, and are treated the same way as pedestrians.

Section 508. Transvestites

For the purposes of this Act, the term "disabled" or "disability" shall not apply to an individual solely because that individual is a transvestite.

Section 509. Coverage of Congress and the Agencies of the Legislative Branch

(a) Coverage of the Senate.

(1) Commitment to Rule XLII. The Senate reaffirms its commitment to Rule XLII of the Standing Rules of the Senate which provides as follows:

"No member, officer, or employee of the Senate shall, with respect to employment by the Senate or any office thereof

"(a) fail or refuse to hire an individual;

"(b) discharge an individual; or

"(c) otherwise discriminate against an individual with respect to promotion, compensation, or terms, conditions, or privileges of employment

on the basis of such individual's race, color, religion, sex, national origin, age, or state of physical handicap.".

(2) Application to Senate Employment. The rights and protections provided pursuant to this Act, the Civil Rights Act of 1990, the Civil Rights Act of 1964, the Age Discrimination in Employment Act of 1967, and

the Rehabilitation Act of 1973 shall apply with respect to employment by the United States Senate.

(3) Investigation and Adjudication of Claims. All claims raised by any individual with respect to Senate employment, pursuant to the Acts referred to in paragraph (2), shall be investigated and adjudicated by the Select Committee on Ethics, pursuant to S. Res. 338, 88th Congress, as amended, or such other entity as the Senate may designate.

(4) Rights of Employees. The Committee on Rules and Administration shall ensure that Senate employees are informed of their rights under the Acts referred to in paragraph (2).

(5) Applicable Remedies. When assigning remedies to individuals found to have a valid claim under the Acts referred to in paragraph (2), the Select Committee on Ethics, or such other entity as the Senate may designate, should to the extent practicable apply the same remedies applicable to all other employees covered by the Acts referred to in paragraph (2). Such remedies shall apply exclusively.

(6) Matters Other Than Employment.

(A) In General. The rights and protections under this Act shall, subject to subparagraph (B), apply with respect to the conduct of the Senate regarding matters other than employment.

(B) Remedies. The Architect of the Capitol shall establish remedies and procedures to be utilized with respect to the rights and protections provided pursuant to subparagraph (A). Such remedies and procedures shall apply exclusively, after approval in accordance with subparagraph (C).

(C) Proposed Remedies and Procedures. For purposes of subparagraph (B), the Architect of the Capitol shall submit proposed remedies and procedures to the Senate Committee on Rules and Administration. The remedies and procedures shall be effective upon the approval of the Committee on Rules and Administration.

(7) Exercise of Rulemaking Power. Notwithstanding any other provision of law, enforcement and adjudication of the rights and protections referred to in paragraphs (2) and (6)(A) shall be within the exclusive jurisdiction of the United States Senate. The provisions of paragraph (1), (3), (4), (5), (6)(B), and (6)(C) are enacted by the Senate as an exercise of the rulemaking power of the Senate, with full recognition of the right of the Senate to change its rules, in the same manner, and to the same extent, as in the case of any other rule of the Senate.

(b) Coverage of the House of Representatives.

(1) In General. Notwithstanding any other provision of this Act or of law, the purposes of this Act shall, subject to paragraphs (2) and (3), apply in their entirety to the House of Representatives.

(2) Employment in the House.

(A) Application. The rights and protections under this Act shall, subject to subparagraph (B), apply with respect to any employee in an employment position in the House of Representatives and any employing authority of the House of Representatives.

(B) Administration.

(i) In General. In the administration of this paragraph, the remedies and procedures made applicable pursuant to the resolution described in clause (ii) shall apply exclusively.

(ii) Resolution. The resolution referred to in clause (i) is House Resolution 15 of the One Hundredth First Congress, as agreed to January 3, 1989, or any other provision that continues in effect the provisions of, or is a successor to, the Fair Employment Practices Resolution.

(C) Exercise of Rulemaking Power. The provisions of subparagraph (B) are enacted by the House of Representatives as an exercise of the rulemaking power of the House of Representatives, with full recognition of the right of the House to change its rules, in the same manner, and to the same extent as in the case of any other rule of the House.

(3) Matters Other Than Employment.

(A) In General. The rights and protections under this Act shall, subject to subparagraph (B), apply with respect to the conduct of the House of Representatives regarding matters other than employment.

(B) Remedies. The Architect of the Capitol shall establish remedies and procedures to be utilized with respect to the rights and protections provided pursuant to subparagraph (A). Such remedies and procedures shall apply exclusively, after approval in accordance with subparagraph (C).

(C) Approval. For purposes of subparagraph (B), the Architect of the Capitol shall submit proposed remedies and procedures to the Speaker of the House of Representatives. The remedies and procedures shall be effective upon the approval of the Speaker, after consultation with the House Office Building Commission.

(c) Instrumentalities of Congress.

(1) In General. The rights and protections under this Act shall, subject to paragraph (2), apply with respect to the conduct of each instrumentality of the Congress.

(2) Establishment of Remedies and Procedures by Instrumentalities. The chief official of each instrumentality of the Congress shall establish remedies and procedures to be utilized with respect to the rights and protections provided pursuant to paragraph (1). Such remedies and procedures shall apply exclusively.

(3) Report to Congress. The chief official of each instrumentality of the Congress shall, after establishing remedies and procedures for purposes of paragraph (2), submit to the Congress a report describing the remedies and procedures.

(4) Definition of Instrumentalities. For purposes of this section, instrumentalities of the Congress include the following: the Architect of the Capitol, the Congres-

sional Budget Office, the General Accounting Office, the Government Printing Office, the Library of Congress, the Office of Technology Assessment, and the United States Botanic Garden.

(5) Construction. Nothing in this section shall alter the enforcement procedures for individuals with disabilities provided in the General Accounting Office Personnel Act of 1980 and regulations promulgated pursuant to that Act.

Section 509 provides that the ADA applies in its entirety to Congress, and provides an enforcement mechanism for the House of Representatives.

Section 510. Illegal Use of Drugs

(a) In General. For purposes of this Act, the term "individual with a disability" does not include an individual who is currently engaging in the illegal use of drugs, when the covered entity acts on the basis of such use.

(b) Rules of Construction. Nothing in subsection (a) shall be construed to exclude as an individual with a disability an individual who

(1) has successfully completed a supervised drug rehabilitation program and is no longer engaging in the illegal use of drugs, or has otherwise been rehabilitated successfully and is no longer engaging in such use;

(2) is participating in a supervised rehabilitation program and is no longer engaging in such use; or

(3) is erroneously regarded as engaging in such use, but is not engaging in such use;

except that it shall not be a violation of this Act for a covered entity to adopt or administer reasonable policies or procedures, including but not limited to drug testing, designed to ensure that an individual described in paragraph (1) or (2) is no longer engaging in the illegal use of drugs; however, nothing in this section shall be construed to encourage, prohibit, restrict, or authorize the conducting of testing for the illegal use of drugs.

(c) Health and Other Services. Notwithstanding subsection (a) and section 511(b)(3), an individual shall not be denied health services, or services provided in connection with drug rehabilitation, on the basis of the current illegal use of drugs if the individual is otherwise entitled to such services.

[A] current illegal user of drugs cannot be refused service at a hospital for a broken leg if that individual is otherwise entitled to that service.

(d) Definition of Illegal Use of Drugs.

(1) In General. The term "illegal use of drugs" means the use of drugs, the possession or distribution of which is unlawful under the Controlled Substances Act. Such term does not include the use of a drug taken under supervision by a licensed health care professional, or other uses authorized by the Controlled Substances Act or other provisions of Federal law.

(2) Drugs. The term "drug" means a controlled substance, as defined in schedules I through V of section 202 of the Controlled Substances Act.

Section 511. Definitions

(a) Homosexuality and Bisexuality. For purposes of the definition of "disability" in section 3(2), homosexuality and bisexuality are not impairments and as such are not disabilities under this Act.

(b) Certain Conditions. Under this Act, the term "disability" shall not include

(1) transvestism, transsexualism, pedophilia, exhibitionism, voyeurism, gender identity disorders not resulting from physical impairments, or other sexual behavior disorders;

(2) compulsive gambling, kleptomania, or pyromania; or

(3) psychoactive substance use disorders resulting from current illegal use of drugs.

Sexual preference is not considered a disability under the ADA, and has not been considered a handicap under the Rehabilitation Act. Individuals who are homosexual or bisexual and are discriminated against because they have a disability, such as infection with the Human Immunodeficiency Virus, are protected under the ADA.

These conditions [in section 511(b)] are physical or mental impairments and would have been included under the ADA, but for this provision.

Section 512. Amendments to the Rehabilitation Act

(a) Definition of Handicapped Individual. Section 7(8) of the Rehabilitation Act of 1973 is amended by redesignating subparagraph (C) as subparagraph (D), and by inserting after subparagraph (B) the following subparagraph:

"(C)(i) For purposes of title V, the term 'individual with handicaps' does not include an individual who is currently engaging in the illegal use of drugs, when a covered entity acts on the basis of such use.

"(ii) Nothing in clause (i) shall be construed to exclude as an individual with handicaps an individual who

"(I) has successfully completed a supervised drug rehabilitation program and is no longer engaging in the illegal use of drugs, or has otherwise been rehabilitated successfully and is no longer engaging in such use;

"(II) is participating in a supervised rehabilitation program and is no longer engaging in such use; or

"(III) is erroneously regarded as engaging in such use, but is not engaging in such use;

except that it shall not be a violation of this Act for a covered entity to adopt or administer reasonable policies or procedures, including but not limited to drug testing, designed to ensure that an individual described in subclause (I) or (II) is no longer engaging in the illegal use of drugs.

"(iii) Notwithstanding clause (i), for purposes of programs and activities providing health services and services provided under titles I, II, and III, an individual shall not be excluded from the benefits of such programs or activities on the basis of his or her current illegal use of drugs if he or she is otherwise entitled to such services.

"(iv) For purposes of programs and activities providing educational services, local educational agencies may take disciplinary action pertaining to the use or possession of illegal drugs or alcohol against any handicapped student who currently is engaging in the illegal use of drugs or in the use of alcohol to the same extent that such disciplinary action is taken against nonhandicapped students. Furthermore, the due process procedures at 34 CFR 104.36 shall not apply to such disciplinary actions.

"(v) For purposes of sections 503 and 504 as such sections relate to employment, the term 'individual with handicaps' does not include any individual who is an alcoholic whose current use of alcohol prevents such individual from performing the duties of the job in question or whose employment, by reason of such current alcohol abuse, would constitute a direct threat to property or the safety of others.".

(b) Definition of Illegal Drugs. Section 7 of the Rehabilitation Act of 1973 is amended by adding at the end the following new paragraph:

"(22)(A) The term 'drug' means a controlled substance, as defined in schedules I through V of section 202 of the Controlled Substances Act.

"(B) The term 'illegal use of drugs' means the use of drugs, the possession or distribution of which is unlawful under the Controlled Substances Act. Such term does not include the use of a drug taken under supervision by a licensed health care professional, or other uses authorized by the Controlled Substances Act or other provisions of Federal law.".

(c) Conforming Amendments. Section 7(8)(B) of the Rehabilitation Act of 1973 is amended

(1) in the first sentence, by striking "Subject to the second sentence of this subparagraph," and inserting "Subject to subparagraphs (C) and (D),"; and

(2) by striking the second sentence.

This section makes amendments to the Rehabilitation Act to exclude protection for current illegal users of drugs when discrimination occurs on that basis, but to protect persons who are not current illegal users of drugs, and have been or are being rehabilitated, or are erroneously regarded as being illegal users of drugs. The Rehabilitation Act presently protects these individuals against discrimination as long as they are qualified to participate in the activity at issue or are qualified to perform the job and do not present a direct threat to property or the safety of others.

[T]he Rehabilitation Act is also amended to provide that if an individual is otherwise entitled to health services, or services provided under titles I, II and III of the Rehabilitation Act, that individuals cannot be denied such services on the basis of current illegal use of drugs.

[T]he Rehabilitation Act is further amended regarding the ability of local education agencies to take disciplinary action based on the current illegal use of drugs or alcohol. Further, the amendment includes a provision regarding alcoholics whose current use of alcohol prevents them from performing the duties of the job in question or whose employment, by reason of the current alcohol abuse, would constitute a direct threat to the health or safety of others.

Section 513. Alternative Means of Dispute Resolution

Where appropriate and to the extent authorized by law, the use of alternative means of dispute resolution, including settlement negotiations, conciliation, facilitation, mediation, factfinding, minitrials, and arbitration, is encouraged to resolve disputes arising under this Act.

[T]he use of alternative dispute resolution mechanisms is intended to supplement, not supplant, the remedies provided by this Act. Thus, for example, the House Committee believes that any agreement to submit disputed issues to arbitration, whether in the context of a collective bargaining agreement or in an employment contract, does not preclude the affected person from seeking relief under the enforcement provisions of this Act.

Section 514. Severability

Should any provision in this Act be found to be unconstitutional by a court of law, such provision shall be severed from the remainder of the Act, and such action shall not affect the enforceability of the remaining provisions of the Act.

SOURCES AND RESOURCES

Sources

The Legislative Process

U.S. Senate, *S. 933, The American with Disabilities Act*, introduced May 5, 1989

U.S. House of Representatives, *H.R. 2237, The American with Disabilities Act*, introduced May 5, 1989

U.S. Senate, *S. 933 Hearings*, Committee on Labor and Human Resources, Subcommittee on the Handicapped, May 9, 1989

U.S. Senate, *S. 933, Report No. 101-116*, Committee on Labor and Human Resources, August 30, 1989

U.S. House of Representatives, *H.R. 2273 Hearings*, Committee on Public Works and Transportation, Subcommittee on Surface Transportation, September 20, 26, 1989

U.S. House of Representatives, *H.R. 2273, Report No. 101-485(I)*, Committee on Public Works and Transportation, May 14, 1990

U.S. House of Representatives, *H.R. 2273 Hearings*, Committee on Education and Labor, Subcommittee on Select Education, August 28, 1989

U.S. House of Representatives, *H.R. 2273 Hearings*, Committee on Education and Labor, Subcommittees on Employment Opportunities and Select Education, September 13, 1989

U.S. House of Representatives, *H.R. 2273 Hearings*, Committee on Education and Labor, Subcommittee on Select Education, October 6, 1989

U.S. House of Representatives, *H.R. 2273, Report No. 101-485(II)*, Committee on Education and Labor, May 15, 1990

U.S. House of Representatives, *H.R. 2273 Hearings*, Committee on the Judiciary, Subcommittee on Civil and Constitutional Law, August 3, October 11, 12, 1989

U.S. House of Representatives, *H.R. 2273, Report No. 101-485(III)*, Senate Committee on the Judiciary, May 15, 1990

U.S. House of Representatives, *H.R. 2273 Hearings*, Committee on Energy and Commerce, Telecommunications Subcommittee, September 27, 1989

U.S. House of Representatives, *H.R. 2273 Hearings*, Committee on Energy and Commerce, Transportation Subcommittee, September 28, 1989

U.S. House of Representatives, *H.R. 2273, Report No. 101-485(IV)*, Committee on Energy and Commerce, May 15, 1990

U.S. Senate, *S. 933, The American with Disabilities Act*, passed, September 7, 1989

U.S. House of Representatives, *H.R. 2237, The American with Disabilities Act*, passed May 22, 1990

U.S. House of Representatives, *S. 933, First House/Senate Conference Report No. 101-558*, June 26, 1990

U.S. House of Representatives, *S. 933, Final House/Senate Conference Report No. 101-596*, July 12, 1990

S. 933, The Americans With Disabilities Act, passed, in lieu of H.R. 2237, July 13, 1990

S. 933, The Americans With Disabilities Act, signed into law, 26 Weekly Compilation of Presidential Documents 1165, July 26, 1990

Americans With Disabilities Act (1990), Public Law 101-336

Americans With Disabilities Act (1990), 104 U.S. Statutes at Large 327

Americans With Disabilities Act (1990), Title 42 United States Code, Sec. 12101

U.S. House of Representatives, *Legislative History of Public Law 101-336, The Americans with Disabilities Act*, 3 vols., December 1990.

Reports

National Council on the Handicapped, *Toward Independence*, February 1986

National Council on the Handicapped, *On The Threshold Of Independence*, January 1988

Presidential Commission on the Human Immunodeficiency Virus Epidemic, *Report on the HIV Epidemic*, 1988

References To U.S. Laws

Administrative Procedures Act (1946)

Age Discrimination in Employment Act (1967)

Air Carrier Access Act (1986)

Civil Rights Act (1964)

Civil Rights Attorney's Fees Awards Act (1976)

Civil Rights Restoration Act (1987)

Civil Rights Act (1990)

Communications Act (1934)

Controlled Substances Act (1970)

Drug Free Workplace Act (1988)

Education Amendments (1972)

Fair Housing Amendments Act (1988)

Federal Railroad Safety Act (1970)

Internal Revenue Code (1986)

Rail Passenger Service Act (1970)

Rehabilitation Act (1973)

Wilderness Act (1964)

Resources

For information about ADA requirements affecting employment, contact:

Equal Employment Opportunity Commission
1801 L Street, N.W.
Washington, DC 20507
(202) 663-4900 (Voice); (800) 800-3302 (TDD);
(202) 663-4494 (TDD for 202 Area Code)

For information about ADA requirements affecting public accommodations and state and local government services, contact:

Department of Justice
Office on the Americans with Disabilities Act
Civil Rights Division
P.O. Box 66118
Washington, DC 20035-6118
(202) 514-0301 (Voice); (202) 514-0381 (TDD)
(202) 514-6193 (Electronic Bulletin Board)

For information about ADA requirements for accessible design in new construction and alterations, contact:

Architectural and Transportation
 Barriers Compliance Board
1111 18th Street, N.W., Suite 501
Washington, DC 20036
(800) USA-ABLE; (800) USA-ABLE (TDD)

For information about ADA requirements affecting transportation, contact:

Department of Transportation
400 Seventh Street, S.W.
Washington, DC 20590
(202) 366-9305; (202) 755-7687 (TDD)

For information about ADA requirements for telecommunications, contact:

Federal Communications Commission
1919 M Street, N.W.
Washington, DC 20554
(202) 632-7260; (202) 632-6999 (TDD)

For information about federal disability-related tax credits and deductions for business, contact:

Internal Revenue Service
Department of the Treasury
1111 Constitution Avenue, N.W.
Washington, DC 20044
(202) 566-2000

(TDD = Telecommunications Device for the Deaf)

INDEX

ALSO AVAILABLE FROM EXCELLENT BOOKS

LANDMARK DECISIONS OF THE UNITED STATES SUPREME COURT
Maureen Harrison & Steve Gilbert, Editors

The actual text of 32 Landmark Decisions of the United States Supreme Court, carefully edited into non-legalese for the general reader, in three volumes.

Vol. I - Includes **Roe** (Abortion), **Brown** (School Desegregation), **Bakke** (Affirmative Action), **The Pentagon Papers** (Press Censorship), **Gideon** (Fair Trials), plus major Landmark Decisions on obscenity, school prayer, sexual privacy, book banning, and flag burning. "Especially important for students." - *The Bookwatch.* "Exactly what you're looking for." - *Wilson Library Bulletin.* "Demystifies the writings of the Court." - *Curriculum Review.*

Vol. II - Includes **Dred Scott** (Slavery) and **Miranda** (Rights of the Accused), plus major Landmark Decisions on women's suffrage, WWII's Japanese American Concentration Camps, Bible reading in the public schools, the book banned in Boston, the death penalty, homosexuality, offensive speech, and the right to die. "Remarkable." - *Booklist.*

Vol. III - Includes **Marbury** (Executive Privilege), **The Scottsboro Boys** (Mob Justice), and **Scopes** (Monkey Trials), plus major Landmark Decisions on the limits of free speech, forced sterilization, the Pledge of Allegiance, illegal search and seizure, interracial marriage, sexual harassment, and Church and State. "Especially recommended." - Midwest Book Review.

ORDER FORM

(Please xerox this form so it will be available to other readers.)

Please send _____ copy(ies) of THE ADA HANDBOOK
_____ copy(ies) of LANDMARK DECISIONS
_____ copy(ies) of LANDMARK DECISIONS II
_____ copy(ies) of LANDMARK DECISIONS III

OUR GUARANTEE: Any Excellent Book may be returned at any time for any reason and a full refund will be made.

Name:_____

Address:_____

City:_____ **State:** _____ **Zip:** _____

Price: $15.95 for THE ADA HANDBOOK
$14.95 for LANDMARK DECISIONS
$15.95 for LANDMARK DECISIONS II
$15.95 for LANDMARK DECISIONS III
Add $1 per book for shipping and handling

Sales Tax: California residents add 7.25%

Mail your check or money order to: Excellent Books, Post Office Box 7121, Beverly Hills, California 90212-7121

7702